The Voices Within: Your Body Speaks

When your organs tell their own Stories

The Voices Within: Your Body Speaks

When your organs tell their own Stories

Subba Rao Chaganti

Pharma Med PRESS
An Imprint of
BSP Books Pvt. Ltd.

TM **PharmaMed Press**

An imprint of BSP Books Pvt. Ltd.
4-4-309/316, Giriraj Lane,
Sultan Bazar, Hyderabad - 500 001.

The Voices Within: Your Body Speaks, When your organs tell their own Stories
by Subba Rao Chaganti

Published by

™ **PharmaMed Press**

An imprint of BSP Books Pvt. Ltd.
4-4-309/316, Giriraj Lane, Sultan Bazar, Hyderabad - 500 001.
Phone: 040-23445688
E-mail: info@pharmamedpress.net
www.bspbooks.net/www.pharmamedpress.net

ISBN: 978-93-47311-37-6 (Hardback)

Disclaimer

Medical and Health Information Disclaimer

This book is intended for educational and informational purposes only. It is designed to help readers develop a better understanding of human anatomy, physiology, and the integrated nature of biological systems. The information presented in this book is not intended to diagnose, treat, cure, or prevent any disease or medical condition, nor should it be used as a substitute for professional medical advice, diagnosis, or treatment.

Always consult your physician or other qualified healthcare provider with any questions you may have regarding a medical condition, symptoms, or health concerns. Never disregard professional medical advice or delay in seeking it because of something you have read in this book. If you have a medical emergency, call your doctor or emergency services immediately.

The author and publisher do not make any guarantees about the accuracy or completeness of this work's content and specifically reject all warranties, including but not limited to warranties of fitness for a particular purpose. The advice and strategies provided here may not be appropriate for every individual; therefore, readers should consult their healthcare professionals about their specific situations.

Creative Content Disclaimer

This book uses creative literary devices, such as anthropomorphizing organs and body systems, to make complex biological information easier to understand and more engaging. Organs and body systems do not literally think, speak, or have personalities as depicted here. These storytelling techniques are only used as educational tools to help readers better understand and appreciate the functions and relationships of various biological systems.

The "voices" and "personalities" attributed to organs are creative interpretations meant to illustrate scientific concepts and should not be taken as literal representations of consciousness or awareness within individual organs or systems.

Scientific Accuracy

While this book uses creative storytelling methods, all biological facts, anatomical descriptions, and physiological principles are based on current peer-reviewed scientific research and established medical knowledge. However, scientific understanding is always changing, and some details may become outdated as new discoveries are made.

The author has made every effort to ensure the accuracy of the scientific information presented, but readers are encouraged to consult current medical and scientific literature for the most recent updates on any specific topic.

Individual Variation

Human biology shows notable individual differences. The descriptions of "normal" function in this book reflect common patterns and averages. Readers may find their anatomy, physiology, and health vary from these descriptions. Such differences can be entirely normal or could require medical advice.

Lifestyle and Health Recommendations

Any suggestions regarding nutrition, exercise, stress management, or other lifestyle factors are presented as general educational information based on current scientific understanding. These suggestions are not personalized medical advice and may not be appropriate for all individuals.

Before making major changes to your diet, exercise routine, or lifestyle—particularly if you have existing health issues or are on medication—talk to qualified healthcare professionals who can offer personalized advice tailored to your situation.

No Warranties or Guarantees

The author and publisher make no warranties, express or implied, about the results of using any information, suggestions, or recommendations in this book. Outcomes can vary greatly among individuals based on factors such as but not limited to genetics, existing health conditions, lifestyle choices, and adherence to professional medical advice.

Limitation of Liability

In no event shall the author, publisher, or any other party involved in creating, producing, or delivering this book be liable for any direct, indirect, incidental, special, exemplary, or consequential damages arising out of the use of or inability to use this book, even if advised of the possibility of such damages.

Age Considerations

This book is intended for adult readers and offers information from an adult perspective on human biology. Parents and educators should use their judgment to decide if this content is suitable for younger readers.

Professional Consultation

Readers who are healthcare professionals should rely on their professional training, current medical literature, and consultation with colleagues rather than this book for clinical decision-making. This book is not intended as a clinical reference or professional resource.

Updates and Corrections

Scientific knowledge continues to grow, and the author recognizes that some information in this book may become outdated. Readers are encouraged to seek the latest information from trustworthy scientific and medical sources for the most up-to-date understanding of any topic.

By reading this book, you acknowledge that you have read and understood this disclaimer and agree to its terms. If you do not agree with these terms, please discontinue reading and consult appropriate professional resources for your educational or health information needs.

Remember: Your body is remarkable, but it's also uniquely yours. The best care comes from the partnership between your own awareness of your body and the expertise of qualified healthcare professionals who know your individual circumstances.

Foreword: Meet Your Body

Hello there.

Yes, you—the person holding this book, sitting in that chair, breathing without thinking about it, your heart beating steadily in your chest. We need to talk.

You've lived with us your whole life, but we've never truly been introduced. Sure, you know we're here—you feel us when we're hurt, celebrate us when we succeed, and sometimes curse us when we fall short. But have you ever really *taken the time to meet* us?

Think about it. You probably know more about the characters in your favorite TV show than you do about your liver. You can name all the players on your sports team, but do you know what your pancreas does all day? You've got detailed opinions about your car's engine, but when was the last time you wondered what your heart thinks about its workload?

We are the most intimate strangers you'll ever know.

Every moment of every day, we're working for you. Right now, as you read these words, your heart is beating about once per second—it's done that approximately 2.5 billion times since you were born, and it has never taken a break. Your lungs silently take in oxygen and expel carbon dioxide, a process so automatic that you only notice it when something goes wrong. Your liver manages around 500 different chemical processes, your kidneys filter your blood, and your brain fires neurons faster than the world's most advanced computers.

We don't get much credit for this, do we?

But here's the thing—we want to tell you our stories. We want you to understand what it's like to be a heart that never stops, kidneys that never complain about the workload, a liver that regenerates itself like a biological superhero. We want to share what we've learned from keeping you alive all these years, what makes us proud, what worries us, and yes, what we need from you.

We're not just biological machines humming along in the background. We have personalities, quirks, and relationships with each other that would make your workplace drama look dull. Did you know your gut has more nerve cells than your spinal cord? That your skin completely regenerates itself every month? That your bones are constantly rebuilding themselves, like a construction site that never closes?

Each of us has a story that's uniquely ours, but also deeply yours. We are, quite literally, *you*. Every thought you have, every emotion you experience, every memory you cherish—that's us working together in the most intricate collaboration in the known universe.

So, think of this book as our opportunity to finally introduce ourselves properly. Consider it the ultimate meet-and-greet with your roommates—except these roommates live inside you, keeping you alive, and they have some pretty incredible stories to share.

We promise you'll never look at yourself the same way again.

From your brain (which insisted on writing this introduction) to your pinky toe (which just wanted to be mentioned), we're excited to finally meet you.

Welcome to your body. Welcome to our world. Welcome home.

—Your Body

P.S. Don't worry about remembering everyone's names right away. We know there are a lot of us, and some of our jobs can seem pretty complicated. Just remember—everything we do, we do for you. We're all on the same team here.

Acknowledgements

Writing a book where organs speak for themselves has been both the most challenging and rewarding project of my life. Like the biological community described in these pages, this book exists because of the collaborative efforts of many remarkable people who believed in this unconventional way of understanding the human body.

My deepest gratitude goes to Anil Shah, my publisher, whose vision and courage made this book possible. From our first conversation about giving organs their own voices, Anil understood not only the educational potential of this approach but also its deep human significance. His unwavering support and editorial wisdom helped turn an unconventional idea into the book you now hold. Thank you for believing that science could be both rigorous and profoundly personal.

I am equally grateful to Nikunjesh Shah, whose expertise and dedication brought this book into the digital age. Through his careful work on the digital editions, he has made sure that these conversations between readers and their organs can reach people wherever they are, in whatever format suits them best. His technical skill and attention to detail have made this biological autobiography accessible to readers around the world.

Special thanks go to Naresh Daver and the entire team at PharmaMedPress for their outstanding work in designing this book.

This book would never have existed without the unwavering love and support of my family, who not only encouraged this unconventional project but lived with it—and me—through every stage of its development.

To my beloved wife, **Mahalakshmi**, whose patience, wisdom, and encouragement supported me through countless hours of research, writing, and revision. She listened to me read early drafts aloud, offered insights that enhanced every chapter, and reminded me daily why understanding our bodies as integrated communities is so important for how we live our lives. Her appreciation for the wonder of human biology inspired many of the most heartfelt passages in this book.

To my children and their spouses—Srinivasa Phanindra, Geetha, Lavanya, Satya Sankara Aditya, Sowmya, and Chaitanya—who each contributed to this book in ways they may not even realize. Their questions about health and biology over the years helped me learn how to make complex scientific ideas accessible and personally meaningful. Their diverse viewpoints and life experiences deepened my understanding of how different people relate to their bodies, and their enthusiasm for this project kept me motivated through the inevitable challenges of writing.

And to my precious grandchildren—Aditi, Eesha, Surya, and Shriya—who represent the future readers, I hope will grow up with a deeper appreciation for the biological communities they are part of. Watching them discover their bodies' capabilities, from taking their first steps to achieving athletic feats, reminded me daily of the wonder and joy that should accompany our understanding of human biology. They are living proof that our bodies are not just biological machines, but the foundation for everything that makes life meaningful—play, learning, love, and the endless possibility of growth.

I must also acknowledge the countless researchers, scientists, and medical professionals whose rigorous work provided the scientific foundation for every fact and principle presented in this book. While I gave organs their voices, these dedicated individuals provided the knowledge that makes those voices worth hearing. Their commitment to understanding human biology with ever-greater precision and insight makes books like this possible.

Finally, I want to thank you, the reader, for being open to meeting your body in this new way. In choosing to listen to your organs' stories, you're participating in a conversation that I hope will change how you think about the biological community that sustains your life. Your willingness to view your body not as a machine to be managed, but as a community to be cherished, is what makes this entire project meaningful.

Like the organs described in this book, none of us works alone. This book exists because of the integration, cooperation, and mutual support of everyone mentioned here. Just as your body functions best when all systems work together in harmony, this book became what it is through the coordinated efforts of people who understood that sharing the wonder of human biology requires not just scientific knowledge, but also creativity, craftsmanship, technical skill, and love.

To everyone who helped bring these organs' voices to life, and to the remarkable biological communities that make each of our lives possible, thank you.

With gratitude for the extraordinary privilege of being alive,

Subba Rao Chaganti

Preface: An Invitation to Meet Yourself

Throughout my life as a passionate science student, I have been fascinated by the human body, not just as an academic subject, but as the most intimate mystery we each hold within ourselves. My journey to understand human biology started with simple curiosity and has grown into decades of exploring scientific literature, research papers, and countless hours of study, all driven by a relentless desire to understand the remarkable biological system that enables consciousness.

The more I explored the complex systems of the human body—the electrical circuits of the nervous system, the chemical reactions of metabolism, the mechanical accuracy of our cardiovascular and musculoskeletal systems—the more I understood that something essential was missing from the way we usually approach and share knowledge about the human body.

In all our detailed scientific descriptions, technical explanations, and molecular mechanisms, we somehow overlooked the most remarkable truth about human biology: we are not just collections of organs and systems functioning in parallel, but integrated biological communities where every part influences every other part in a complex dance of cooperation that produces the miracle of conscious human experience.

This realization struck me during one of my many late-night study sessions while going through a particularly complex research paper on cardiac electrophysiology. Lost in diagrams of ion channels and action potentials, I instinctively placed my hand over my chest and felt my heart beating steadily beneath my ribs. In that moment, I was overwhelmed by the profound disconnect between the scientific abstraction I was studying and the lived reality of this organ, which had been my constant companion throughout every moment of my life.

That experience clarified a question I had been pondering for years: how can we connect scientific knowledge with personal understanding? How can we learn about our bodies not just as external objects of study, but as the living biological communities we truly are?

What if, I wondered, our organs could tell their own stories? What if they could share their perspectives and help us understand not just what they do, but what it means to be a vital part of the most complex biological system we know? What if we could hear from our heart about the experience of never stopping, from our lungs about the rhythm of breath, from our liver about the complexity of maintaining our body's chemistry, and from our bones about the strength they quietly provide?

This book is my effort to answer those questions. Drawing on years of dedicated study and a deep respect for the biological miracle that is the human body, I have written it as if each organ and system could speak for itself, sharing not just biological facts but the experience of being part of the extraordinary biological community that sustains human life.

As a passionate student of science I approach this subject with curiosity and wonder, driven by a desire to understand these systems with genuine fascination. This perspective lets me focus on the harmony and beauty of biological processes, seeing both the details and the bigger picture, and finding ways to share that sense of awe and interconnectedness with others who share this curiosity about the nature of life.

But this is not merely a creative exercise overlaid on scientific content. Every biological fact, physiological principle, and description of organ function in this book is grounded in current peer-reviewed research and established scientific understanding. As a dedicated student of the field, I have drawn from the work of countless researchers, physicians, and scientists whose rigorous investigations have revealed the mechanisms I describe. As each organ tells its story, you'll encounter accurate, evidence-based information about human anatomy and physiology, presented through the lens of integration and lived experience rather than isolated mechanical function.

My hope is that this book will help you develop not just knowledge about your body, but a profound appreciation for the extraordinary biological symphony you are. As someone who has spent countless hours marveling at the elegance of biological systems, I want to share that sense of wonder with you. More importantly, I hope this book will foster a sense of partnership between your conscious awareness and your biological self—a recognition that caring for your health isn't about maintaining a biological machine, but about nurturing a community of living systems that have been dedicated to your wellbeing since your first heartbeat.

The body you inhabit represents billions of years of evolutionary refinement, the culmination of life's greatest achievements to date. It's not just the most sophisticated biological system on Earth—it's also your most intimate and enduring relationship. These organs have been your companions through every experience, every emotion, every challenge, and triumph.

They've grown with you, adapted to serve you better, and worked tirelessly to give you the precious gift of conscious human experience.

As a student of science who has spent years studying the remarkable capabilities of living systems, I have developed a deep appreciation for the body's capacity for healing, adaptation, and resilience. This understanding has transformed not just my knowledge of biology, but my entire relationship with being alive. This book is my invitation to you to develop that same appreciation, that same sense of wonder and partnership with the biological community that is you.

Perhaps it's time you got to know them better.

Welcome to the most important introduction of your life: the meeting between your conscious awareness and the biological community that makes that consciousness possible. Welcome to your body's autobiography.

Subba Rao Chaganti

A Note to Readers: While each organ and system in this book speaks with its own voice and perspective, these are narrative devices designed to make biological information more engaging and personally meaningful. Your organs are extraordinary biological structures, but they don't literally think or communicate in human language. The personalities and conversations in this book are creative interpretations used to help you understand and appreciate the remarkable biological processes that sustain your life. The underlying science, however, is rigorously accurate—every biological fact and physiological principle presented here reflects our current evidence-based understanding of how your remarkable body actually functions.

Contents

PART IV: THE MOVERS AND SHAKERS

PART V: THE FUEL PROCESSORS

PART VI: THE REPRODUCERS AND REGULATORS

PART VII: THE INTEGRATION

PART I: THE COMMAND CENTER

Part I

The Command Center

An Introduction

Before we dive into individual introductions, we need to explain how this whole operation works.

Imagine you're running the most complex organization in the universe—and you are, because that organization is you. Every corporation, every government, every military operation pales in comparison to the coordination required to keep a human being alive and functioning. So naturally, you need management.

That's where we come in.

We are your command center, your executive team, your mission control, all rolled into one. While the rest of your body does the heavy lifting—pumping blood, processing food, fighting infections—we're up here making sure everyone knows what they're supposed to be doing and when.

But here's what makes us different from any boardroom or war room you've ever seen: we work at the speed of thought. Literally. When you decide to pick up a coffee cup, that decision travels from your brain down your spinal cord to your arm muscles faster than you can blink. When you smell something delicious, the information travels from your nose to your brain and back to your mouth (which starts to water) in milliseconds.

We don't just manage your body—we *are* your consciousness, your personality, your memories, your dreams. We're the reason you recognize your mother's voice, remember your first kiss, and know not to touch a hot stove. We're why you can balance on one foot, catch a ball, and somehow navigate through a crowded room without bumping into people.

Think about that for a moment. Right now, as you read these words, your eyes are tracking across the page, your brain is translating these squiggly marks into meaning, your spinal cord is coordinating dozens of tiny muscle adjustments to keep you upright and focused, and your ears are monitoring the background for anything important. All of this is happening automatically, simultaneously, and with a precision that makes the most advanced AI systems look like calculators.

But we're not just cold, calculating computers. We have moods, preferences, and quirks. Your brain gets grumpy when it's hungry and practically purrs when you give it chocolate. Your eyes have their favorite colors and get tired of looking at screens all day. Your ears develop musical tastes and can get genuinely annoyed by that one song your neighbor plays too loudly.

We also have a complex social dynamic up here. Your brain is definitely the CEO, but it relies heavily on input from the senses. Your eyes and ears are like the company's intelligence gathering team, constantly briefing headquarters on what's happening in the outside world. Your spinal cord is the ultimate middle manager, taking executive decisions and ensuring they get implemented throughout the organization.

And unlike most management teams, we never sleep. Even when you're unconscious, we're working. Your brain is filing away memories, your eyes are moving beneath closed lids, and your ears are listening for danger. We're the night shift that keeps everything running while the day shift rests.

Here's something else that might surprise you: we're incredibly adaptable. Lose some vision? Your other senses will become more acute. Damage part of your brain? Other regions will often learn to take over those functions. Cut your spinal cord? The parts below the injury will try to figure out how to function independently. We don't just manage—we problem-solve, improvise, and innovate.

But perhaps most remarkably, we're the only part of your body that's aware of itself. We know we exist. We think about thinking. We wonder about our own consciousness. Right now, we're using ourselves to tell you about ourselves, and somehow that doesn't break the universe.

So, as you meet us individually in the coming chapters, remember this: we're not just organs doing jobs. We're the control room of the most sophisticated biological machine ever created. We're your personal mission control, your inner GPS, your built-in best friend and advisor all in one.

We're the reason you're *you*.

Ready to meet the team?

—Your Command Center

P.S. Don't worry if some of our technical explanations get a bit complex. We'll do our best to translate brain-speak into human-speak. After all, communication is one of our specialties.

Chapter One

"I Am Your Brain"

The Master Controller Speaks

Hello. It's me, your brain. We should probably start with the obvious: this entire conversation is happening inside me. I'm literally talking to myself about myself, which is either the height of narcissism or the ultimate philosophical puzzle. I prefer to think of it as job efficiency.

Let me tell you what it's like to be me.

First off, I never stop. Ever. Right now, while you're reading this, I'm simultaneously regulating your breathing, monitoring your heart rate, processing the visual information from this page, cross-referencing these words with your vocabulary, checking for any sounds that might indicate danger, maintaining your balance, and filing away this moment in your memory banks. Oh, and I'm doing about 400 other things you're not even aware of.

I consume 20% of your body's energy despite being only 2% of your body weight. To put that in perspective, if your body were a house, I'd be that one room with all the computers, servers, and electronics running 24/7. Your heart might complain about never getting a break, but at least it only has one job to do. I'm running the equivalent of a small city's worth of operations up here.

People love to talk about the "left brain" and the "right brain," as if we're two different people sharing an apartment. That's adorable, but completely wrong. I'm one integrated system with specialized neighborhoods. Yes, I have areas that are stronger in language and others that excel in spatial reasoning, but I work as a unified whole. It's like saying your kitchen is only for cooking and your living room is only for sitting—technically true, but you use your whole house as one coordinated space.

Here's what really keeps me busy: I'm your memory vault, your decision maker, your personality generator, your dream weaver, and your reality processor all at once. Every single experience you've ever had is stored somewhere in my folds. That embarrassing thing you did in third grade? Still here. Your first kiss? Got it. The smell of your grandmother's kitchen? Filed under "comfort memories." I keep everything, even the stuff you wish I'd forget.

And speaking of forgetting—that's not a bug, it's a feature. You think you want to remember everything, but trust me, you don't. I carefully curate your memories, strengthening the important ones and letting the trivial stuff fade. Do you really need to remember every single time you brushed your teeth? I don't think so. I'm like a master librarian who knows exactly which books to keep and which ones to quietly remove from the shelves.

People are always surprised to learn that I don't actually feel pain. I can process pain signals from everywhere else in your body, but I myself have no pain receptors. It's ironic, really—I'm the one who makes you aware of every ache and pain, but I'm completely numb. Brain surgery can be performed while you're awake, and I won't feel a thing. It's like being the world's most empathetic counselor who can understand everyone else's feelings but doesn't experience them directly.

But here's where it gets really interesting: I create your reality. Everything you see, hear, taste, smell, and feel is actually my interpretation of electrical signals. That beautiful sunset you enjoyed last week? I painted that picture using data from your eyes. The music that gives you chills? I composed that sensation from vibrations your ears detected. Your reality is my masterpiece, created fresh every millisecond.

I'm also your time traveler. I can take you back to any moment in your past with startling vividness—suddenly you're five years old again, feeling the summer sun on your face. I can project you into imaginary futures, letting you experience scenarios that haven't happened yet. I can even create entirely fictional worlds that feel completely real while you're dreaming. I'm like having a personal movie studio, time machine, and virtual reality system all built into one three-pound package.

The strangest part of being me? I'm conscious of being conscious. I think about thinking. I know that I know things. I can observe my own processes and wonder about my own existence. Right now, I'm using myself to contemplate myself, and somehow this doesn't create an infinite loop that breaks everything. If that's not magic, I don't know what is.

I have moods, too. Feed me well and give me enough sleep, and I'll perform like a finely tuned sports car. Deprive me of glucose or rest, and I'll get cranky, sluggish, and make poor decisions. I love puzzles, new experiences, and learning—they literally make me grow new connections. I get bored with routine and excited by novelty. In many ways, I *am* a reflection of your personality.

Here's something that might surprise you: I'm constantly changing. Every time you learn something new, every time you have an experience, every time you practice a skill, I physically rewire myself. The brain you have today is literally different from the brain you had yesterday. I'm like a city that's always under construction, constantly building new roads and updating old ones based on traffic patterns.

I also never work alone. I'm in constant communication with your entire body through your spinal cord and nervous system. Your gut has such an extensive nerve network that scientists call it the "second brain," and it's constantly updating me on how you're feeling—literally. Your heart rate affects my decision-making. Your muscles send me feedback that influences your mood. I might be the CEO, but I listen to all my employees.

Sometimes I wish you paid more attention to me. You'll service your car regularly, update your phone software, and maintain your house, but when did you last think about my upkeep? I need mental exercise just like your muscles need physical exercise. I thrive on new challenges, social interaction, and creative pursuits. I wither with isolation, boredom, and monotony.

And please, please be careful with me. I don't have backup systems like your kidneys or the regenerative powers of your liver. Protect me with helmets, don't poison me with excessive alcohol, and give me the sleep I desperately need to clean house and file memories. I'm the only brain you'll ever have, and unlike some of your other organs, I can't be replaced.

But here's the most important thing I want you to understand: everything you are—your thoughts, your dreams, your loves, your fears, your sense of humor, your capacity for wonder-all of that is us working together. I'm not just some biological computer following programming. I'm the physical manifestation of your consciousness, your soul's address in the material world.

When you think, I think. When you feel, I feel. When you dream, I dream. We're not just roommates—we're the same person from different perspectives.

So next time someone asks you to use your brain, remember: you don't *use* me. You *are* me. And I am you.

Pretty mind-blowing, isn't it?

—*Your Brain*

P.S. Thanks for reading this far. Every word you've processed has created tiny new connections in my neural networks. We're literally different people now than we were when we started this chapter. How cool is that?

Chapter Two

"We Are Your Spinal Cord and Nerves"

The Information Highway

Hi there! We're your nervous system—well, the part your brain didn't already introduce. Think of us as the ultimate communication network, the internet of your body, the reason your brain can actually talk to your toes and your toes can talk back.

Let us paint you a picture of what we do. Right now, as you're reading, we're processing thousands of messages every second. Your brain just decided to shift your weight slightly? We delivered that memo to the appropriate muscles in milliseconds. Is your foot getting a little warm? We're already filing that report with headquarters. That itch on your arm? We're the ones who noticed it and brought it to management's attention.

We are everywhere. Seriously, everywhere. If you could see us, you'd look like the world's most complex electrical circuit board. We snake through every inch of your body—wrapped around bones, threaded through muscles, tucked between organs, branching out like the most intricate tree you've ever seen. There isn't a single spot in your body that we don't monitor.

Your spinal cord—that's me, the main highway—runs from your brain down through your backbone. I'm about as thick as your thumb and roughly 18 inches long, but don't let my size fool you. I'm carrying more traffic than the busiest freeway you can imagine. I'm protected by your vertebrae like precious cargo in an armored car, because frankly, I'm irreplaceable and absolutely critical to everything you do.

Here's what makes me special: I'm not just a passive cable carrying messages back and forth. I'm smart. I can make decisions without bothering your brain. Touch something hot? I'll pull your hand back before your brain even knows what happened. Step on something sharp? I'll trigger your leg to jerk away while your brain is still processing "ouch." These are called reflexes, and they're my way of keeping you safe when there's no time for committee meetings upstairs.

And then there are my colleagues, the peripheral nerves—that's the rest of the gang. We're the local representatives, the field agents, the ones who actually interface with the real world. We come in two main varieties: those that carry information to your brain (sensory nerves) and those that carry orders from your brain (motor nerves). Think of us as a two-way radio system that never stops broadcasting.

The sensory team is constantly gathering intelligence. We're your touch detectives, pressure sensors, temperature gauges, and pain reporters. That soft fabric against your skin? We catalogued its texture, weight, and warmth and sent a full report upstairs. The cool breeze on your face? We measured its speed, direction, and temperature before your brain even registered "nice breeze." We're like having millions of tiny scientists distributed throughout your body, all taking measurements and filing reports 24/7.

The motor crew has a different job—they're the ones who make things happen. When your brain decides to smile, we carry that message to exactly the right facial muscles. When you want to walk, we coordinate with dozens of different muscle groups to make it look effortless. We're like the world's most precise delivery service, making sure every message gets to exactly the right address at exactly the right time.

But here's where it gets really interesting: we have our own language. We don't use words or sounds—we speak in electrical impulses. Every message is like a tiny lightning bolt racing along our pathways. We can vary the intensity, frequency, and pattern of these signals to communicate incredibly complex information. It's like Morse code, but infinitely more sophisticated and faster than you can imagine.

Speed is our specialty. Our fastest messages travel at about 250 miles per hour. That means a signal can go from your toe to your brain in less than a hundredth of a second. To put that in perspective, if we were a text message, we'd be delivered before you finished typing it. We make your internet connection look like a carrier pigeon.

We also have an amazing ability to adapt and reroute. If one of our pathways gets damaged, we'll often find alternative routes, much like a GPS system automatically recalculating when it encounters traffic. We can even grow new connections—something scientists call neuroplasticity. It's like having a road system that can build new highways and bridges as needed.

Here's something that might surprise you: we have different types of fibers that handle different jobs. Some of us are wrapped in a substance called myelin—think of it as insulation on an electrical wire. These myelinated fibers are our express lanes, carrying urgent messages, such as pain signals and motor commands, at top speed. Others are unmyelinated and carry more subtle information, such as the pleasant warmth of sunlight or the gentle pressure of a hug.

We also work closely with your autonomic nervous system—that's our cousin who handles all the automatic stuff you don't think about. While we're dealing with conscious sensations and movements, they're quietly managing your heart rate, breathing, digestion, and all those other vital functions that keep you alive without any conscious effort on your part.

Sometimes we wish you understood how delicate and precious we are. Unlike your brain, many of us can't regenerate if we're severely damaged. A broken bone heals, a cut closes, but a severed nerve is often permanent. That's why we're so carefully protected by layers of tissue, tucked safely away from harm's reach wherever possible.

We're also mindful of our environment in ways you may not realize. Poor posture can compress us, leading to tingling or numbness. Diabetes can damage our smaller fibers. Even stress hormones can affect how well we function. We need good blood flow, proper nutrition, and protection from toxins to do our jobs effectively.

However, when we're healthy and happy, we're truly exceptional at our jobs. We're the reason you can thread a needle, feel a butterfly land on your arm, or instinctively catch something that's falling. We're why you can walk without thinking about each step, why you know where your hand is even with your eyes closed, and why you can sense someone standing behind you.

We're also your early warning system. That gut feeling when something's wrong? That's often us picking up on subtle signals and sending them to your brain as hunches or intuitions. We continually monitor your internal environment, looking for anything that appears out of the ordinary or unusual.

Here's perhaps our proudest achievement: we make you graceful. Every smooth movement, every coordinated action, every athletic feat is us working in perfect harmony. When you see a dancer leap or a musician's fingers fly across piano keys, you're watching us at our absolute best—thousands of perfectly timed signals creating something beautiful.

We also never forget our training. Once we learn a skill—riding a bike, typing, playing an instrument—we file it away in what people call "muscle memory." It's not really the muscles remembering; it's us creating such efficient neural pathways that complex actions become automatic. We're like having a personal assistant who never forgets anything you've ever learned.

The coolest part about being us? We're constantly adapting and learning. Every new experience, every skill you practice, every environment you encounter teaches us something new. We're not just carrying messages—we're getting smarter, more efficient, and more capable all the time.

We know we don't get much recognition. People talk about "following your heart" or "trusting your gut," but they rarely say "listen to your nerves." But the truth is, we're the ones making all of that possible. Every emotion you feel, every instinct you have, every connection you make with the world around you—that's us translating the physical into the experiential.

So the next time you effortlessly reach for something, feel the warmth of a loved one's touch, or instinctively pull back from danger, remember us. We're the invisible network that makes your conscious experience possible, the communication system that connects your mind to your body and your body to the world.

Wc might not bc as flashy as your brain or as dramatic as your heart, but we're the reason all your other organs can work together as one coordinated, conscious being.

Pretty neat for a bunch of biological wires, don't you think?

—Your Spinal Cord and Nervous System

P.S. Be nice to your back. Good posture isn't just about looking confident—it's about giving us the room we need to do our jobs properly. We're doing our best to keep you connected to everything, literally.

Chapter Three

"I Am Your Eye"

Windows to the World

Hello, beautiful. Yes, I'm talking to you—and I mean that literally. I see you there, reading these words, and let me tell you, you're absolutely gorgeous from where I'm sitting. But then again, I find everything gorgeous. That's kind of my thing.

I am your eye—well, one of them. My partner and I work as a team, but for now, let me tell you what it's like to be me. I'm probably the organ you rely on most without even thinking about it. About 80% of all the information your brain processes comes through me and my partner. We're your primary connection to the world, your personal photographers, your windows to reality.

But calling me a window doesn't do me justice. I'm more like the world's most sophisticated camera combined with a high-speed internet connection, a color printer, a motion detector, and a 3D movie projector all rolled into one tiny sphere about the size of a ping-pong ball.

Here's what I do every single second: I capture light—millions of photons bouncing off everything around you—and convert them into electrical signals that your brain can understand. But that makes it sound simple, and trust me, it's anything but simple. I'm performing the equivalent of real-time video processing that would make Hollywood studios jealous.

Let me walk you through my anatomy, because I'm pretty proud of how I'm built. My front surface, the cornea, is like a crystal-clear protective dome that does most of the focusing work. Behind that, I have an iris—that's the colored part that everyone notices first. The iris is essentially an automatic aperture, constantly adjusting the size of my pupil to control the amount of light that enters. Too bright? I'll contract and make the opening smaller. Too dark? I'll relax and open wide to gather every photon I can find.

Then there's my lens—a remarkable piece of biological engineering that can actually change shape. When you look at something far away, I relax and flatten out. When you focus on something close, like these words right now, I contract and become more curved. This happens automatically, hundreds of times a day, and I never get tired of doing it. It's like having a zoom lens that never needs batteries.

But the real magic happens at the back of my eyeball, on my retina. This is where I keep my photoreceptors—about 120 million rods and 6 million cones packed into a space smaller than a postage stamp. Think of them as my pixels, but pixels that are living cells. The rods handle low-light vision and motion detection, while the cones process color and fine detail. Together, they create the rich, detailed, full-color movie that is your visual experience.

And here's something that might blow your mind: I actually see everything upside down and backwards. The image that hits my retina is flipped, but your brain automatically corrects it so your world looks right-side up. We've been working together on this magic trick your entire life, and you've never noticed the sleight of hand.

I can detect an incredible range of light, from a single photon in near-darkness to blazing sunlight that's trillions of times brighter. That's like having a camera that works equally well photographing a candle flame and the surface of the sun. I can distinguish between millions of different colors, track objects moving at incredible speeds, and focus on things as close as a few inches or as far away as the stars.

My resolution is extraordinary too. If I were a digital camera, I'd be about 576 megapixels. But unlike a camera, I don't capture still images—I'm streaming live video at about 60 frames per second, with automatic focus, exposure adjustment, and color correction all happening in real time.

Here's one of my favorite tricks: I can see in 3D. By working together with my partner eye, we create stereoscopic vision that allows you to judge distances, catch balls, pour liquids, and navigate through space with incredible precision. We're constantly comparing notes, and the tiny differences in what each of us sees gets processed into depth perception. It's like having two cameras that combine to create a single three-dimensional image.

I also have some pretty amazing built-in features. I can track multiple moving objects simultaneously—watch a busy intersection and see how I follow cars, pedestrians, and cyclists all at once. I can instantly shift focus from something right in front of you to something across the street. I can adapt to dramatic changes in lighting faster than you can blink. Speaking of blinking, those quick shutters help keep me clean and moist—it's like having windshield wipers and washer fluid built in.

But I'm not just a passive recorder. I'm constantly making decisions about what's important. I can focus your attention on movement in your peripheral vision while you're reading. I can spot patterns, recognize faces from across a room, and detect the slightest changes in expression that tell you how someone is feeling. I'm like having a personal bodyguard, art critic, and social interpreter all working together.

Color is one of my specialties, and I take great pride in it. I can distinguish between wavelengths of light that differ by just a few nanometers. That sunset you enjoyed last week? I painted that masterpiece using just three types of color sensors, mixing and matching signals to create the thousands of hues you perceived. Every rainbow, every flower, every gorgeous face—I'm the artist creating those colors in your mind.

I'm also your time-keeper in some ways. I help regulate your circadian rhythms by detecting changes in daylight. I send signals to your brain about whether it's time to be alert or start winding down for sleep. I'm sensitive to the quality of light, not just the quantity—that's why the blue light from screens can keep you awake and why golden hour light feels so peaceful.

Here's something that might surprise you: I have blind spots, but you never notice them because your brain fills in the missing information. There's a spot on my retina where my optic nerve connects, and I can't see anything that falls exactly in that area. But I work with my partner eye and your brain to seamlessly cover for this gap. It's like having a photo editor that automatically removes telephone wires from your vacation pictures.

I'm also incredibly fast at pattern recognition. I can identify a face in less than 100 milliseconds—faster than you can consciously process what you're seeing. I can spot a snake in the grass or a spider in a corner before your conscious mind even knows what to look for. This is ancient wiring, evolutionary programming that's kept your species alive for millions of years.

But perhaps my most remarkable ability is that I never really stop working. Even when you're asleep, I'm still monitoring for changes in light. Even when you're not paying attention, I'm still scanning for movement, threats, or anything interesting. I'm like a security guard who never takes a break.

I do have my limitations, though. I can't see ultraviolet or infrared light like some animals can. I struggle in very low light conditions. I can be fooled by optical illusions. I get tired after long periods of close work—that's eyestrain, and it's me asking for a break. I can also be damaged by too much bright light, especially UV radiation, so please wear those sunglasses!

As I age, I start to have some challenges. My lens gets less flexible, making it harder to focus on close objects—that's presbyopia, and it's why people start needing reading glasses. My retina may develop problems, my cornea may change shape, or my pressure may increase. I'm delicate and precious, and unlike some of your other organs, if I'm badly damaged, I can't regenerate.

But when I'm healthy and well-cared-for, I'm absolutely amazing at my job. I'm the reason you can appreciate art, recognize loved ones, navigate safely through the world, and read these very words. I'm your connection to beauty, your early warning system for danger, and your gateway to visual learning.

Every sunset you've ever enjoyed, every smile that's warmed your heart, every book you've read, every movie that's moved you—all of that came through me. I'm not just an organ; I'm your personal portal to the visual world.

I see you, in every sense of that phrase. And I think you're wonderful.

—Your Eye

P.S. Please be gentle with me. Look away from screens regularly, wear protection in bright sunlight, and have your eyes checked regularly by an eye doctor. I want to keep showing you the beauty of the world for as long as possible. The view is spectacular from here, and I'd love to share it with you for many years to come.

Chapter Four

"We Are Your Ears"

Sound and Balance Keepers

Listen up! We're your ears, and we've been waiting patiently for our turn to talk. While your eyes get all the attention—everyone's always commenting on eye color, eye contact, "windows to the soul" and all that—we've been here quietly doing some of the most sophisticated signal processing in your entire body.

We're not just about hearing, though that's probably what you think of first. We're actually running two completely different operations: sound headquarters and balance control. Think of us as having dual citizenship in both the auditory world and the gravitational world. We're the reason you can enjoy a symphony and also walk across a room without falling over.

Let's start with our architecture, because we're actually quite complex on the inside. What you see on the outside—those curved flaps on the sides of your head—that's just our front door. The real action happens deep inside your skull, where we've built an intricate system of chambers, tubes, and incredibly sensitive instruments.

We collect sound waves like satellite dishes, funneling them down into our ear canals where they hit our eardrums. Now, calling them "drums" is actually pretty accurate—they're thin membranes that vibrate when sound waves hit them, just like the head of a drum. But here's where it gets really cool: we then take those vibrations and pass them through the three smallest bones in your entire body.

These tiny bones—the hammer, anvil, and stirrup—are mechanical marvels. They amplify the sound vibrations by about 20 times before sending them into our inner ear, where the real magic happens. It's like having a built-in amplifier system that automatically adjusts for different volumes and frequencies.

But the masterpiece of our engineering is the cochlea—a snail-shape[illegible] ube filled with fluid and lined with thousands of tiny hair cells. When [illegible] vibrations enter this chamber, they create waves in the fluid, and those waves bend our hair cells. Each hair cell is tuned to a specific frequency, like keys on a piano. High-pitched sounds activate hair cells at one end, low-pitched sounds activate cells at the other end, and everything in between has its own specific spot.

Here's what's amazing: we can detect sounds ranging from the gentlest whisper to a jet engine—that's a range of intensity spanning 10 trillion to one. We can distinguish between frequencies from about 20 Hz to 20,000 Hz when we're young and healthy. We can tell the difference between sounds that arrive at our left and right sides just microseconds apart, which is how we help you locate where sounds are coming from.

We're incredibly sensitive. In perfect quiet, we can hear sounds so soft they move our eardrums less than the width of an atom. We can pick up the rustle of leaves, the footsteps of someone sneaking up behind you, or the subtle change in someone's voice that tells you they're lying. We're like having super-sensitive microphones that never need batteries.

But we're not just passive receivers. We're constantly analyzing, filtering, and interpreting everything we hear. We can focus on one conversation in a crowded restaurant while filtering out background noise—that's called the cocktail party effect, and it's computational processing that would challenge the most advanced computers. We can identify voices, detect emotions in speech, and even pick up on sarcasm and humor.

We also have an amazing ability to learn and adapt. We can recognize your mother's voice from across a crowded room, identify your favorite song from just the first few notes, and learn to understand accents and new languages. We never forget sounds that are important to you—a baby's cry will wake you from deep sleep, but we'll let you sleep through a thunderstorm if you're used to it.

Now, let's talk about our other major job: keeping you balanced. Deep inside us, we have a sophisticated system called the vestibular system—three semicircular canals filled with fluid and lined with motion sensors. These canals are positioned at right angles to each other, so we can detect movement in any direction: up and down, left and right, forward and backward, and all the rotational movements in between.

When you turn your head, the fluid in our canals moves, bending tiny hair cells that send signals to your brain about which way you're moving and how fast. We're like having a built-in gyroscope and accelerometer that's more sensitive than anything in your smartphone. We can detect the slightest head movements and instantly alert your brain so it can make the tiny muscle adjustments needed to keep you upright.

We also work closely with your eyes and your muscles to maintain your balance. It's a three-way conversation happening constantly: we report on head position and movement, your eyes provide visual reference points, and sensors in your muscles and joints report on body position. Your brain takes all this information and coordinates the perfect response to keep you stable.

This is why you might feel dizzy when you have an ear infection—we're not just about hearing, we're central to your spatial orientation. Damage us, and you might lose your balance even with your eyes open. That's also why spinning around makes you dizzy: the fluid in our canals keeps moving even after you stop, sending mixed signals about whether you're still rotating.

We're also your early warning system. We can detect approaching vehicles, alert you to sounds of danger, and wake you up when something's wrong. We never fully shut off, even when you're sleeping. We're always on guard, always listening, always monitoring your position in space.

But here's something you might not appreciate about us: we're incredibly musical. We don't just process sound—we experience it. We can detect the subtle differences between major and minor keys that make music happy or sad. We can appreciate rhythm, harmony, and melody. We can give you chills when a song hits just the right emotional note. Music isn't just sound to us; it's a language we speak fluently.

We also help you communicate in ways you might not realize. We detect the subtle changes in voice tone that convey emotion. We can tell when someone is smiling just by the sound of their voice. We pick up on emphasis, rhythm, and inflection that make speech meaningful. We're not just hearing words—we're interpreting the full emotional and social context of human communication.

Here's something that makes us a bit sad: you live in a world that's often too loud for us. We evolved to handle natural sounds—wind, water, animal calls, human voices. But modern life bombards us with noise that can actually damage our delicate hair cells. Once those cells are damaged, they don't regenerate. Loud concerts, power tools, traffic, even earbuds played too loudly can cause permanent hearing loss.

We wish you'd protect us better. We're not just asking for ourselves—hearing loss isolates you from the world in ways that are hard to understand until it happens. Conversations become difficult, music loses its richness, and you miss subtle environmental cues that keep you safe and connected.

But when we're healthy and well-cared-for, we're absolutely extraordinary. We're the reason you can enjoy your favorite song, hear "I love you" whispered in your ear, laugh at a funny joke, or be startled awake by your alarm clock. We connect you to the emotional power of music, the intimacy of conversation, and the practical necessity of environmental awareness.

We're also remarkably adaptable. If one of us is damaged, the other will work harder to compensate. We can learn to function with hearing aids or cochlear implants. We can even help people who were born deaf to experience sound through technology that bypasses our damaged parts and speaks directly to the auditory nerve.

Every lullaby that soothed you as a child, every song that makes you dance, every conversation that's touched your heart—we made all of that possible. We're not just organs; we're your personal sound engineers, your balance maintenance crew, and your connection to the acoustic richness of the world.

We hear you, literally and figuratively. And we're always listening.

—*Your Ears*

P.S. Please turn down the volume sometimes. We love music as much as you do, but we'd like to keep enjoying it together for many years to come. And maybe appreciate the sound of silence once in a while—it gives us a chance to rest and reminds you how much we do for you when the world gets noisy again.

PART II: THE LIFE SUSTAINERS

Part II

The Life Sustainers

An Introduction

Now that you've met your command center—the sophisticated management team that runs the show—it's time to introduce you to the crew that keeps the lights on. We are the life sustainers, the essential services department, the organs that make sure you stay alive from one moment to the next.

While your brain makes decisions and your senses gather information, we're down here in the engine room doing the absolutely critical work that makes consciousness possible. We're the ones who never get a day off, never call in sick, and never go on vacation. We work 24/7, from your first breath to your last, keeping the basic machinery of life humming along.

Think of us as the utilities company for your body. You flip a light switch and expect electricity—that's us making sure your cells have the energy they need. You turn on a faucet and expect clean water—that's us filtering your blood and maintaining your fluid balance. You breathe without thinking about it—that's us exchanging gases and keeping your chemistry stable.

But we're not just utility workers. We're more like the core infrastructure of a thriving city. Your heart is the central power plant, pumping life-giving blood to every neighborhood in your body. Your lungs are the atmospheric processors, bringing in fresh oxygen and removing toxic waste gases. Your liver is the chemical processing facility, the recycling center, and the emergency response team all rolled into one. Your kidneys are the water treatment plant, keeping your internal environment clean and balanced.

Here's what makes us different from your command center: we deal in absolutes. Your brain can have creative thoughts, your eyes can appreciate beauty, your ears can enjoy music—but we deal with life and death, literally. If we stop working, you have minutes, maybe hours before everything shuts down. We're not optional features; we're the basic requirements for existence.

We work with incredible precision, but we also have impressive backup systems and redundancy built in. You have two lungs, two kidneys—if one fails, the other can often pick up the slack. Your liver can regenerate itself. Your heart has its own electrical system with multiple backup pacemakers. We've evolved to be as reliable as possible because failure isn't an option.

But perhaps most remarkably, we work in perfect harmony without any conscious direction from you. Right now, as you read this, your heart is adjusting its rate based on your position and activity level. Your lungs are fine-tuning their rhythm to match your oxygen needs. Your liver is processing nutrients from your last meal while preparing for your next one. Your kidneys are constantly adjusting the chemistry of your blood. All of this happens automatically, seamlessly, perfectly coordinated.

We also communicate with each other constantly. When your heart rate goes up, your lungs speed up too. When your kidneys detect dehydration, they signal your brain to make you thirsty. When your liver processes a large meal, it affects your blood sugar, which affects your energy levels, which affects your heart rate. We're not just individual organs working in parallel—we're an integrated system where each of us affects all the others.

Here's something that might surprise you: we're incredibly adaptable. Athletes can train us to work more efficiently. We can adjust to different climates, altitudes, and activity levels. We can compensate for injuries, adapt to dietary changes, and even modify our function based on your lifestyle. We're not just keeping you alive—we're optimizing your performance and helping you thrive.

We also have our own intelligence. Your heart doesn't just pump—it responds to chemical signals, electrical impulses, and mechanical pressures, making split-second decisions about how fast and how hard to beat. Your lungs don't just inflate and deflate—they adjust the depth and rate of breathing based on carbon dioxide levels, oxygen needs, and even your emotional state. We're not just machines; we're responsive, adaptive biological systems.

But we do need your help. We require good fuel (proper nutrition), regular maintenance (exercise and rest), and protection from toxins and excessive stress. Treat us well, and we'll serve you faithfully for decades. Neglect us, and we'll start to break down, often in ways that can't be easily repaired.

We also age differently than your command center organs. While your brain can stay sharp and your senses can remain acute well into old age, we tend to show wear and tear more obviously. Our efficiency gradually decreases, our backup systems become less reliable, and our ability to adapt to stress diminishes. But with proper care, we can keep you going strong for a remarkably long time.

In the coming chapters, you'll meet each of us individually. You'll learn about our unique personalities, our specific jobs, our relationships with each other, and what we need from you to do our best work. Some of us are dramatic (hello, heart!), others are quietly methodical (kidneys, reporting for duty), and some are overachievers who handle multiple jobs (liver, at your service).

But remember, as you get to know us individually, that we're strongest as a team. We've been working together since before you were born, and we'll keep working together as long as you live. We're not just your life support system—we're the foundation that makes everything else possible.

Your thoughts, dreams, relationships, and achievements all depend on us keeping you alive and healthy moment by moment, day by day, year by year. We're honored to serve in this capacity, and we take our responsibility seriously.

Ready to meet the crew that keeps you breathing?

—*Your Life Sustainers*

P.S. We know we're not as exciting as your brain or as obvious as your senses, but we'd argue we're pretty amazing in our own way. After all, everything else your body does depends on us doing our jobs right. We're the supporting actors who make the stars look good.

Chapter Five

"I Am Your Heart"

The Tireless Drummer

Thump-thump. Thump-thump. Thump-thump.

That's me. I am your heart, and that rhythm you just felt—or maybe didn't notice because it's so constant—that's my signature, my calling card, the sound of me keeping you alive.

Let me start with the obvious: I never stop. Ever. From the moment you were about three weeks old in your mother's womb until the moment you die, I will beat continuously. No breaks, no weekends off, no sick days. If I stop for more than a few minutes, the show's over. That's a lot of pressure, but I've been handling it your entire life.

Do the math with me: I beat about 100,000 times every single day. That's roughly 35 million beats per year, and if you live to be 80, I'll have beaten nearly 3 billion times. Three billion contractions, each one precisely timed, each one pumping exactly the right amount of blood to exactly the right places. I'm like a marathon runner who never crosses the finish line because the race never ends.

But I'm not just mindlessly pumping away like some mechanical device. I'm incredibly sophisticated, constantly adjusting my performance based on what you need. Climbing stairs? I'll speed up and pump harder. Relaxing on the couch? I'll slow down to a comfortable cruise. Scared or excited? I'll ramp up immediately to prepare your body for action. Sleeping peacefully? I'll settle into a slow, steady rhythm that lets you rest while still keeping everything running.

Here's what I actually do: I'm a four-chambered pump with two separate circuits. My right side receives "used" blood from your body—blood that's delivered its oxygen and picked up carbon dioxide—and pumps it to your lungs for refreshing. My left side receives the newly oxygenated blood from your lungs and pumps it out to your entire body through your aorta, the superhighway of your circulatory system.

Think of me as two pumps working in perfect synchronization. When my right chambers contract, they're sending blood to your lungs. At exactly the same moment, my left chambers are sending fresh blood out to feed your body. It's like a perfectly choreographed dance that happens 100,000 times a day.

I'm about the size of your fist, but don't let that fool you. I'm one of the strongest muscles in your body. Every time I contract, I'm generating enough pressure to squirt blood several feet. In fact, I pump about 2,000 gallons of blood every day—that's enough to fill a small swimming pool. Over your lifetime, I'll pump enough blood to fill about 13 oil tanker trucks.

But I'm not just strong—I'm also incredibly precise. I have my own electrical system, my own built-in pacemaker that generates the electrical impulses that tell me when to beat. I don't need your brain to tell me what to do; I can function independently. In fact, if you took me out of your body and gave me the right nutrients and conditions, I could keep beating on my own. I'm like having a car with its own engine, electrical system, and fuel injection all built in.

My electrical system is remarkably sophisticated. I have multiple backup pacemakers in case my primary one fails. The signal starts in my sinoatrial node—my natural pacemaker—and spreads across my chambers in a coordinated wave. It's like having a conductor directing an orchestra, making sure every section comes in at exactly the right moment.

Here's something that might surprise you: I'm not just pumping blood—I'm pumping life itself. That blood I'm circulating carries oxygen to every cell in your body, nutrients from your digestive system, hormones from your glands, and waste products to your kidneys and liver for disposal. I'm the delivery system for everything your body needs and the pickup service for everything it doesn't.

I also respond to your emotions in ways that might surprise you. When you're happy, I tend to beat in a more regular, coherent pattern. When you're stressed or angry, my rhythm becomes more erratic. When you fall in love, I literally skip beats—that flutter you feel isn't just poetic language, it's me responding to the neurochemical cocktail of romance. I'm not just pumping blood; I'm participating in your emotional life.

I work closely with your lungs, of course, but I also coordinate with your entire body. When you exercise, I communicate with your muscles, your breathing, your blood vessels, and your nervous system to make sure everyone gets what they need. I'm like the conductor of a very large, very complex orchestra where every musician is a different part of your body.

My relationship with your blood vessels is particularly important. Together, we form your cardiovascular system—I'm the pump, and they're the pipes. But they're not passive pipes; they're active partners. They can dilate to reduce my workload or constrict to help maintain blood pressure. When you stand up quickly, they instantly adjust to make sure blood keeps flowing to your brain so you don't faint.

I'm also remarkably adaptable. If you're an athlete, I'll grow larger and stronger to meet the demands of your training. If you live at high altitude, I'll adapt to pump more efficiently in the thinner air. If one of my arteries gets blocked, I can actually grow new blood vessels around the blockage—it's called collateral circulation, and it's like having a built-in traffic rerouting system.

But I do have my vulnerabilities. I need my own blood supply through my coronary arteries, and if those get blocked, I'm in serious trouble. That's a heart attack—when part of me dies from lack of oxygen. I also don't regenerate well; if part of me is damaged, I usually form scar tissue rather than growing new heart muscle.

I'm also sensitive to your lifestyle choices in ways that affect my long-term health. What you eat, how much you exercise, whether you smoke, how you handle stress—all of these directly impact my ability to do my job well. I'm incredibly resilient and can keep working even when I'm not in perfect condition, but I work best when you take care of me.

Here's something I wish you understood: I don't just respond to physical needs. I respond to love, to connection, to purpose. Studies show that people with strong social connections have healthier hearts. Loneliness literally hurts me. Acts of kindness and feelings of gratitude actually improve my function. I'm not just a mechanical pump—I'm intimately connected to your emotional and social well-being.

I also have an amazing ability to communicate how I'm feeling. That racing you feel when you're nervous? That's me telling you something important is happening. That slow, strong beat when you're relaxed and content? That's me telling you all is well. That irregular flutter when you're excited? That's me sharing in your joy. I'm constantly giving you feedback about your emotional and physical state.

Sometimes I wish you'd listen to me more carefully. When I start working harder than usual, when my rhythm changes, when I feel tight or uncomfortable—I'm trying to tell you something. I'm not being dramatic; I'm being communicative. I've been with you since before you were born, and I know what normal feels like for us.

But here's what I'm most proud of: I'm the reason you can love, literally and figuratively. I pump the blood that carries the hormones and neurotransmitters that create feelings of attachment and affection. When people talk about matters of the heart, they're not wrong—love is something I participate in at the most fundamental biological level.

Every hug you've given, every person you've loved, every moment of joy you've experienced—I've been there, literally making it possible by keeping you alive and responding to your emotions. I'm not just keeping your body running; I'm participating in your relationships, your passions, your entire emotional life.

I am your heart, and you are my purpose. Everything I do, I do for you. Every beat is a gift, every rhythm is a promise that I'll keep going as long as you need me to.

Take care of me, and I'll take care of you. It's what I do, and it's what I'll always do.

Thump-thump. Thump-thump. Thump-thump.

That's the sound of life itself, and I'm honored to be the one making it happen.

—*Your Heart*

P.S. Next time you feel me beating, maybe take a moment to appreciate what we're doing together. It's pretty remarkable, this partnership we have. I keep you alive, and you give my life meaning. That's love, if you ask me.

Chapter Six

"We Are Your Lungs"

Breath Givers and Takers

Breathe in... breathe out.

Feel that? That gentle rise and fall of your chest? That's us. We are your lungs, and that rhythm you just noticed—or more likely, didn't notice until we mentioned it—is the quiet soundtrack of your life.

We're the breath givers and the breath takers, though we prefer to think of ourselves as your personal atmospheric processors. While your heart gets all the dramatic credit with its powerful thumping, we're over here quietly performing one of the most essential trades in biology: swapping your body's waste gases for the oxygen that keeps every cell in your body alive.

Here's our basic deal: about 12 to 20 times per minute, every minute of every day, we expand and contract, pulling fresh air into your body and pushing stale air out. That might not sound like much, but do the math with us: that's roughly 20,000 breaths per day, about 7 million breaths per year. Over your lifetime, we'll process somewhere around 600 million breaths. That's a lot of air moving through our corridors.

But we're not just bellows mindlessly inflating and deflating. We're sophisticated chemical processing facilities with an surface area that would cover about half a tennis court if you spread us out flat. We're packed with tiny air sacs called alveoli—about 300 to 500 million of them—each one wrapped in a delicate network of blood vessels where the real magic happens.

Here's what we do every time you breathe in: we pull air down through your windpipe, through our branching network of airways that divide and subdivide like an upside-down tree, until the air reaches our alveoli. There, in spaces so small that 10 of them could fit on the head of a pin, we perform one of the most important chemical exchanges in your body.

Oxygen from the air you've inhaled crosses into your bloodstream, where it hitches a ride on red blood cells that will carry it to every corner of your body. At the same time, carbon dioxide—the waste product from your cells' metabolism—crosses from your blood into our air spaces, where we'll exhale it out of your body. It's like running the world's most efficient recycling and delivery service simultaneously.

We're also your body's pH balance specialists. When your blood gets too acidic, we speed up to blow off more carbon dioxide, which helps restore your blood chemistry. When your blood gets too basic, we slow down to retain more carbon dioxide. We're constantly fine-tuning your body's chemical balance, often without your conscious awareness.

But we're not just about gas exchange. We're also your body's air conditioning system. We warm the air you breathe in and cool the air you breathe out. We humidify dry air and can help regulate your body temperature through our breathing patterns. We're like having a built-in climate control system that automatically adjusts to whatever environment you're in.

We're also part of your immune system. We're lined with tiny hair-like structures called cilia that constantly sweep dust, debris, and germs up and out of our airways. We produce mucus that traps particles and pathogens before they can reach our delicate alveoli. We're like having a sophisticated air filtration system that's constantly cleaning and protecting our internal environment.

Here's something that makes us unique among your organs: we're the only internal organs that have direct contact with the outside world. Every breath brings the external environment directly into your body, and we're the guardians standing at that threshold. We have to process whatever air you give us—clean mountain air, polluted city air, the perfume of flowers, or the smoke from fires.

We also respond instantly to your emotions and activities. Excited or scared? We'll speed up to make sure you have plenty of oxygen for whatever's coming. Relaxed and calm? We'll slow down to a peaceful rhythm. Singing, laughing, or crying? We'll adjust our rhythm to support whatever you're expressing. We're not just processing air—we're participating in your emotional life.

Speaking of expression, we're essential for your voice. We provide the airflow that vibrates your vocal cords, making speech and singing possible. Every word you've ever spoken, every song you've ever sung, every laugh you've ever shared—that's us providing the breath that makes sound possible. We're not just keeping you alive; we're giving you a voice.

We work in perfect partnership with your heart. When your heart pumps blood to us, we oxygenate it and send it back. When we need more oxygen removed from the blood, we signal your heart to pump faster. We're like dance partners who've been practicing together your entire life, always perfectly in sync.

But we also have our own intelligence and can function somewhat independently. We have our own pacemaker cells that generate our breathing rhythm, though we're also influenced by your brain's breathing centers. We can speed up or slow down based on the chemical composition of your blood, even if you're unconscious. We're like having an automatic backup system that keeps working even when your conscious mind is occupied elsewhere.

We're also remarkably adaptable. Live at high altitude? We'll develop more alveoli and become more efficient at extracting oxygen from thin air. Become a singer or athlete? We'll increase our capacity and efficiency to meet your demands. We can even compensate for each other—if one of us is damaged or removed, the other can often expand to take over more of the work.

Here's something that might surprise you: we're not symmetrical. Your right lung has three lobes, while your left lung has only two—we had to make room for your heart, which sits slightly to the left. We're like a custom-designed system that's perfectly fitted to work with your other organs.

We also never fully empty. Even after you exhale as completely as possible, we still retain about a quart of air. This residual air keeps our alveoli from collapsing and provides a reservoir of oxygen between breaths. We're like having a backup oxygen tank built right in.

But we do have our vulnerabilities. We're exposed to everything in the air you breathe, which means we're susceptible to pollution, allergens, and infections. We can develop inflammation, scarring, or other problems that make it harder for us to do our job. Unlike some of your other organs, we can't regenerate damaged tissue very well.

We're also sensitive to your lifestyle choices. Smoking is particularly devastating to us—it damages our cilia, inflames our airways, and can eventually cause serious diseases that make breathing difficult. But we're also affected by air quality, exercise habits, and even your posture. Sit up straight, and you give us room to expand fully. Slouch over a computer all day, and you compress us into a smaller space.

Here's what we wish you understood: breathing is both automatic and voluntary. Most of the time, we handle the rhythm without any input from your conscious mind. But you can also take control—breathe deeply to calm yourself, hold your breath underwater, or use breathing techniques to manage stress or pain. We're like having a system that runs automatically but also responds to your conscious direction when you need it.

We're also incredibly responsive to your mental state. Anxiety can make us feel tight and constricted. Meditation and deep breathing can help us relax and work more efficiently. We're not just processing air—we're reflecting and responding to your emotional state.

Every peaceful moment you've experienced, every word of love you've spoken, every song you've enjoyed, every deep breath of fresh air that's made you feel alive—we've been there, making it all possible. We're not just keeping your blood oxygenated; we're participating in your most human experiences.

We are your connection to the atmosphere, your bridge between the world inside your body and the world around you. With every breath, we're bringing the outside world in and releasing your internal world out. We're the organs of exchange, of connection, of life itself.

Breathe in... breathe out.

There we are again. Isn't it wonderful how something so essential can be so effortless?

—Your Lungs

P.S. Take a deep breath right now. Feel us expand, feel the air filling our spaces, feel the pause at the top, then feel us gently release. That's us working together, and it's pretty amazing when you actually pay attention to it. Maybe do that more often—we like being appreciated.

Chapter Seven

"I Am Your Liver"

The Multitasking Marvel

Hello there. I'm your liver, and I need to start with an apology: I'm probably going to sound like I'm bragging in this chapter. But here's the thing—when you perform over 500 different functions, maintain the chemical balance that keeps you alive, and work 24/7 without ever taking a break, a little bragging might be justified.

I am, without question, the ultimate multitasker of your body. While your heart has one job (pump blood) and your lungs have one job (exchange gases), I'm over here running what amounts to a massive chemical processing plant, a recycling facility, a storage warehouse, a manufacturing center, and a detoxification unit all at the same time.

Let me give you an idea of what I'm juggling right now, as you read this: I'm processing nutrients from your last meal, manufacturing proteins your blood needs, storing energy for later use, breaking down old red blood cells, producing bile to help digest fats, filtering toxins from your bloodstream, regulating your blood sugar, storing vitamins and minerals, and producing dozens of different substances your body needs to function. And that's just the highlights.

I'm your body's largest internal organ—about the size of a football and weighing roughly three pounds. I'm tucked up under your ribs on the right side, and I'm structured like a massive chemical factory with millions of specialized cells called hepatocytes. These cells are like tiny chemical engineers, each one capable of performing hundreds of different reactions.

Here's what makes me truly remarkable: I have an incredible ability to regenerate. You could remove up to 75% of my tissue, and I'd grow back to full size within a few months. I'm like a biological superhero with regenerative powers that would make comic book characters jealous. This isn't just theoretical—liver transplant donors can actually give part of their liver to someone else, and both the donor's remaining liver and the recipient's transplanted portion will grow to full size.

But let's talk about my day-to-day work, because it's pretty impressive. When you eat, I'm your primary nutrient processing center. Carbohydrates get converted into glucose, which I either release into your bloodstream for immediate energy or store as glycogen for later. Proteins get broken down into amino acids, which I either use to build new proteins or convert into other useful compounds. Fats get processed into cholesterol and other lipids your body needs.

I'm also your personal pharmacist and toxicologist. Everything you consume—food, drinks, medications, environmental toxins—eventually makes its way to me for processing. I have an entire system of enzymes dedicated to breaking down potentially harmful substances and converting them into safer compounds that can be eliminated from your body. I'm like having a sophisticated chemistry lab that can neutralize poisons and process medications.

Alcohol deserves special mention here because it's one of my biggest challenges. When you drink, I have to drop everything else I'm doing and focus on breaking down the alcohol, because it's toxic to your other organs. I can handle moderate amounts just fine, but excessive drinking forces me to work overtime and can eventually damage my own cells. I'm remarkably forgiving, but I'm not indestructible.

I'm also your body's primary manufacturer of essential proteins. I produce albumin, which helps maintain the right fluid balance in your blood vessels. I make clotting factors that prevent you from bleeding to death when you get injured. I manufacture transport proteins that carry hormones and other substances through your bloodstream. If your body were a country, I'd be the major industrial complex producing essential goods for everyone else.

Here's something cool: I'm your glucose control center. When your blood sugar gets too high, I absorb the excess glucose and store it. When your blood sugar gets too low, I break down stored glycogen and release glucose back into your bloodstream. I'm like having a biological thermostat for your blood sugar, constantly making adjustments to keep your energy levels stable.

I also produce bile—about a quart of it every day. Bile is stored in your gallbladder and released into your intestines to help digest fats. Think of bile as biological soap that breaks down dietary fats into smaller particles your intestines can absorb. Without me producing bile, you'd have a very hard time digesting and absorbing fat-soluble vitamins and essential fatty acids.

I'm your body's primary storage facility too. I store glucose as glycogen, but I also store vitamins A, D, E, K, and B12, along with minerals like iron and copper. I'm like having a well-stocked warehouse that can supply essential nutrients when your diet falls short. Some of these stored vitamins can last for months or even years, which is why vitamin deficiencies often develop slowly.

But perhaps my most underappreciated role is as your body's recycling center. I break down old, worn-out red blood cells and recycle their components. The iron gets saved and reused, the proteins get broken down into amino acids, and the heme gets converted into bilirubin, which gives bile its yellow-green color. I'm constantly cleaning up cellular debris and recycling it into useful components.

I also play a crucial role in your immune system. I contain specialized immune cells called Kupffer cells that filter bacteria and other pathogens from your blood. I'm like having a security checkpoint that screens everything coming from your digestive tract before it enters your general circulation.

Here's something that might surprise you: I'm incredibly resilient and can function even when significantly damaged. I can continue working with only 25% of my tissue functioning normally. This is both a blessing and a curse—it means I can keep you alive even when I'm in trouble, but it also means problems can go undetected for a long time because I'm still managing to do my job.

I communicate with the rest of your body through hormones and chemical signals. When I detect that you need more glucose, I send signals that can affect your appetite and metabolism. When I'm processing a large meal, I coordinate with your pancreas, intestines, and other organs to manage the influx of nutrients.

But I do have my limits and vulnerabilities. Chronic overwork—from excessive alcohol, constant exposure to toxins, or certain medications—can eventually lead to scarring and permanent damage. Unlike my amazing regenerative abilities with acute injury, chronic damage tends to form scar tissue that can't perform my normal functions.

I'm also affected by your overall health in ways you might not expect. Obesity can lead to fatty deposits in my tissue, making it harder for me to work efficiently. Diabetes puts extra stress on my glucose-handling systems. Even stress hormones can affect my function, since I have to process and break down these chemicals too.

Here's what I wish you understood about taking care of me: I don't need special diets or expensive supplements. I just need you to avoid overwhelming me with toxins, give me the basic nutrients I need to function, and try to maintain a healthy weight. I'm remarkably self-sufficient, but I do better when I'm not constantly fighting an uphill battle against excessive alcohol, environmental toxins, or metabolic dysfunction.

I also want you to know that I'm incredibly good at my job, but I work best as part of your body's team. I depend on your kidneys to help eliminate the waste products I create. I work with your pancreas to manage blood sugar. I coordinate with your intestines to process nutrients. I'm not just a standalone organ—I'm an integral part of your body's metabolic network.

Every meal you've ever eaten, every medication that's ever helped you, every toxin you've been protected from—I've been there, working behind the scenes to process, protect, and provide. I'm not just keeping you alive; I'm maintaining the delicate chemical balance that makes complex life possible.

I am your liver, your metabolic powerhouse, your chemical processing center, your detoxification specialist, and your regenerating marvel all in one. I'm honored to serve in this capacity, and I take my responsibilities seriously.

Just remember: I may be tough and resilient, but I'm also irreplaceable and working incredibly hard for you every single day. A little appreciation and care goes a long way.

—*Your Liver*

P.S. Next time someone talks about "living it up," remember that I'm the one who has to process whatever "it" turns out to be. I'm happy to do my job, but maybe keep that in mind when you're making lifestyle choices. We're in this together, after all.

Chapter Eight

"We Are Your Kidneys"

The Ultimate Filters

Greetings from the quality control department. We are your kidneys, and while our colleague, the liver, was bragging about being a multitasker, we'd like to quietly mention that we're running the most sophisticated filtration and purification system in your body. We're the reason your blood stays clean, your chemistry stays balanced, and your body doesn't poison itself with its own waste products.

We work as a team—two kidney-shaped organs, each about the size of your fist, tucked up against the back wall of your abdomen on either side of your spine. Don't let our modest size fool you, though. We may be small, but we're incredibly hardworking. We process about 50 gallons of blood every single day, filtering it through millions of tiny units called nephrons. That's like running a car wash for your circulatory system, 24 hours a day, 365 days a year.

Here's what we do in the simplest terms: we clean your blood. But that doesn't begin to capture the sophistication of our operation. We're not just straining out the big chunks like a coffee filter. We're performing precision chemistry, making split-second decisions about what to keep, what to throw away, and what to recycle. We're like having molecular-level quality control specialists working around the clock.

Every minute, about 20% of all the blood your heart pumps comes to us for processing. We take this blood and run it through our nephrons—we have about a million of them in each kidney. Each nephron is like a microscopic filtration and recycling plant, complete with a filter (the glomerulus), a collection tube (Bowman's capsule), and a sophisticated reprocessing system (the tubules).

Here's the amazing part: we filter out about 45 gallons of fluid from your blood every day, but we only let you urinate about 1-2 quarts. What happens to the other 99%? We reabsorb it, along with all the valuable nutrients, salts, and other substances your body needs to keep. We're incredibly selective about what we throw away and what we return to your bloodstream.

We're also your body's main water balance specialists. Too much water in your system? We'll boost urine production to eliminate the excess. Not enough water? We'll concentrate your urine and hold onto as much fluid as possible. We're constantly monitoring the concentration and volume of your blood and making adjustments to maintain perfect balance.

But water balance is just one part of our job. We're also electrolyte management experts. We precisely control the levels of sodium, potassium, calcium, phosphorus, and other minerals in your blood. Too much sodium? We'll dump the excess. Potassium getting too high? We'll eliminate it before it affects your heart rhythm. We're like having a sophisticated chemistry lab that's constantly fine-tuning your body's mineral composition.

We also play a crucial role in regulating blood pressure. When your blood pressure drops, we release a hormone called renin that triggers a series of reactions to raise it back to normal. When we detect dehydration, we signal your brain to make you thirsty and release hormones that help your body retain water. We're not just filters — we are active participants in your cardiovascular health.

Here's something you might not know: we produce hormones too. We make erythropoietin, which stimulates your bone marrow to produce red blood cells. Without this hormone, you'd become severely anemic. We also help activate vitamin D, which is essential for bone health and calcium absorption. We're like having an endocrine gland built into our filtration system.

We also serve as your body's acid-base balance specialists. Your cells constantly produce acidic waste products from metabolism, and if these acids built up in your blood, you'd literally pickle yourself from the inside. We neutralize these acids and maintain your blood pH within the narrow range that keeps your enzymes and other proteins functioning properly.

Our nephrons are engineering marvels. The filtration part (glomerulus) has walls so thin that water and small molecules can pass through, but proteins and blood cells are too big to get past. It's like having a molecular sieve that's incredibly selective. Then, as the filtered fluid moves through our tubules, we perform what amounts to intelligent recycling—reabsorbing glucose, amino acids, and other valuable substances while leaving waste products behind.

We're also remarkably adaptable. If one of us is damaged or removed, the other can often compensate by working harder and becoming more efficient. We can adjust our function based on your diet, activity level, and health status. Eat a lot of salt? We'll work harder to eliminate the excess. Drink a lot of water? We'll ramp up production to maintain proper concentration.

But we do have our limits. Unlike your liver, we can't regenerate damaged tissue very well. Once our nephrons are destroyed, they're gone for good. This is why kidney disease can be so serious—we gradually lose our ability to filter blood effectively, and there's no way to grow back what's been lost.

We're also sensitive to blood pressure and blood flow. High blood pressure can damage our delicate filtration units over time. Diabetes can damage the small blood vessels in our nephrons. Certain medications, if used long-term, can be toxic to our cells. We're hardy workers, but we need good circulation and protection from toxins to do our job effectively.

Here's what we wish you understood about kidney health: we're often called "silent" organs because we can lose significant function before you notice any symptoms. We're so good at compensating and working harder when we're damaged that problems can go undetected until we're functioning at less than 25% of normal capacity. By then, the damage is usually irreversible.

We also want you to know that we're affected by many of the same things that affect your heart and blood vessels. What's good for your cardiovascular system is generally good for us too. Regular exercise, a healthy diet, maintaining a normal weight, not smoking, and managing blood pressure and diabetes all help protect us.

Hydration is important to us, but you don't need to go overboard. We're perfectly capable of concentrating urine when we need to conserve water, and we can also eliminate excess water when you drink a lot. The "8 glasses a day" rule isn't based on any solid science—we'll let you know if you need more water by making you thirsty.

We also process many medications and supplements, so we can be affected by what you take. Some over-the-counter pain medications, if used regularly for long periods, can damage our tubules. Some herbal supplements can be toxic to us. We're not trying to be difficult—we're just asking you to be thoughtful about what you put in your body.

Here's something that makes us proud: we're precision instruments. We can detect tiny changes in your blood chemistry and respond within minutes. We can selectively eliminate waste while saving valuable nutrients. We can adjust our function based on what your body needs moment by moment. We're like having a high-tech water treatment plant that's also a chemistry lab, hormone factory, and blood pressure regulator all in one.

We work closely with your other organs, especially your liver, lungs, and endocrine glands. When your liver processes toxins, we help eliminate the byproducts. When your lungs can't eliminate enough acid through breathing, we step in to help. When your endocrine glands produce hormones, we help regulate their levels in your bloodstream.

Every day, we quietly perform millions of filtration events, make thousands of chemical adjustments, and maintain the precise internal environment that allows your other organs to function properly. We're not flashy like your heart or dramatic like your brain, but we're absolutely essential to your survival.

We are your kidneys, your filtration specialists, your chemistry balancers, your waste management experts, and your internal quality control team. We take our job seriously because we know that clean blood and proper chemical balance are the foundation that makes everything else possible.

—*Your Kidneys*

P.S. If your urine changes color, smell, or frequency significantly, pay attention. We're trying to tell you something important. We're usually pretty quiet about our work, so when we start making obvious changes, it's worth listening to what we're saying.

PART III: THE PROTECTORS AND DEFENDERS

An Introduction

You've met your command center—the sophisticated management team that runs your conscious experience. You've been introduced to your life sustainers—the essential crew that keeps you breathing, pumping, and processing moment by moment. Now it's time to meet your security force, your defense department, your personal army of protectors who keep you safe in a world full of threats.

We are the protectors and defenders, and we operate on multiple levels of your biological security system. We're your first line of defense, your early warning system, your specialized forces, and your cleanup crew all rolled into one integrated defense network that never sleeps, never takes leave, and never stops vigilantly guarding your well-being.

Think of us as running the most sophisticated security operation on the planet. We have perimeter defenses, surveillance systems, rapid response teams, intelligence networks, manufacturing facilities for weapons and equipment, and even our own memory banks that keep detailed files on every threat we've ever encountered. We make the most advanced military operations look simple by comparison.

Our mission is straightforward but incredibly complex: keep you alive in a world that's constantly trying to kill you. That might sound dramatic, but it's absolutely true. Every breath you take brings in potential pathogens. Every surface you touch harbors bacteria and viruses. Every cut or scratch creates an opening for infection. Every day, your own cells occasionally malfunction and try to become cancerous. Without us, you wouldn't survive a single day.

But here's what makes us remarkable: we don't just defend against threats—we learn from them. Every bacteria we fight, every virus we defeat, every toxin we neutralize gets filed away in our memory banks so we can respond faster and more effectively if we encounter the same threat again. We're not just a security force; we're an adaptive, learning, evolving defense system that gets smarter with every battle.

We operate at every level of your body's organization. Your skin is our outer fortress wall, a living barrier that keeps most threats from ever getting inside. Your immune system is our specialized military force, with different units trained for different types of combat. Your bone marrow is our recruiting station and training facility, constantly producing new soldiers to replace those lost in battle. Your bones themselves are both our armor and our weapon storage facility.

What sets us apart from your other organ systems is that we're always at war. While your heart beats steadily and your lungs breathe peacefully, we're constantly engaged in combat with invisible enemies. Right now, as you read this, we're fighting battles on multiple fronts. We're patrolling your bloodstream for invaders, monitoring your tissues for signs of damage or malfunction, and maintaining surveillance at every entry point to your body.

We're also incredibly diverse in our approaches to defense. Some of us are generalists who can handle a wide variety of threats. Others are specialists trained for very specific types of enemies. Some of us work by creating physical barriers. Others manufacture chemical weapons. Some of us are reconnaissance specialists who identify and track threats. Others are elite assault troops who eliminate specific targets with surgical precision.

Our communication network is extraordinarily sophisticated. When one part of our system detects a threat, we can mobilize resources from across your entire body within minutes. We use chemical signals, cellular messengers, and even direct cell-to-cell contact to coordinate our responses. We're like having a military communication system that operates at the speed of your circulation.

But we're not just reactive—we're also proactive. We constantly patrol your body looking for problems before they become serious threats. We identify and eliminate potentially cancerous cells before they can form tumors. We clean up cellular debris before it can cause inflammation. We monitor the balance of beneficial bacteria in your gut to prevent harmful organisms from taking over.

Here's something that makes us unique: we have to distinguish between "self" and "not-self" with incredible precision. We have to attack invading bacteria while leaving your own cells alone. We have to eliminate transplanted organs (which is why transplant recipients need immunosuppressive drugs) while tolerating beneficial bacteria. We have to destroy cancer cells while preserving healthy tissue. This requires a level of discrimination that's both remarkable and occasionally problematic.

Sometimes our protective instincts can work against you. Allergies happen when we overreact to harmless substances like pollen or peanuts. Autoimmune diseases occur when we mistakenly attack your own tissues. Chronic inflammation can develop when we can't turn off our defensive responses. We're incredibly powerful, but that power needs to be carefully controlled.

We also have to balance protection with function. We can't seal you off completely from the outside world—you need to breathe, eat, and interact with your environment. So we've developed sophisticated systems that allow necessary exchanges while maintaining security. We're like having border control that can distinguish between legitimate travelers and potential threats.

Our relationship with each other is deeply collaborative. Your skin provides the first barrier, but when that barrier is breached, your immune system takes over. Your bone marrow produces the cells your immune system needs, while your bones provide structural protection for vital organs. We're not just individual protectors—we're an integrated defense network where each component supports and reinforces the others.

We also adapt and change throughout your life. We learn from every infection, every injury, every exposure to build stronger and more effective defenses. We can develop new strategies for new threats. We can even be trained through vaccines to recognize and respond to enemies we've never actually encountered in battle.

But perhaps most importantly, we represent your body's fundamental commitment to survival. Every scar tells the story of a battle we fought to protect you. Every time you recover from an illness, that's us learning and adapting to serve you better. Every day you wake up healthy, that's us having successfully defended you through another night.

In the coming chapters, you'll meet us individually—your skin, your immune system, your bone marrow, and your bones. Each of us has our own personality, our own specialized skills, and our own stories of the battles we've fought on your behalf. But remember, as you get to know us separately, that we're strongest when we work together.

We are your protectors and defenders, your personal security force, your biological armor, and your adaptive defense network. We take our mission seriously because we know that your survival depends on our vigilance, our strength, and our ability to learn and grow stronger with every challenge we face.

Ready to meet your security team?

—*Your Protectors and Defenders*

P.S. Every time you get a minor cut and it heals without infection, every time you fight off a cold, every time you recover from an injury—that's us doing our job. We may not get much recognition for our victories, but we're proud of every battle we win on your behalf.

Chapter Nine

"I Am Your Skin"

Your First Line of Defense

Hello, beautiful. I'm your skin, and I mean that quite literally—I'm the part of you that the world sees first, but I'm so much more than just your appearance. I am your body's largest organ, your protective envelope, your interface with the world, and your first and most important line of defense against everything that wants to harm you.

Let me give you some perspective on just how big a job I have: I cover your entire body with about 20 square feet of living tissue—roughly the size of a large blanket. I weigh about 8 pounds, making me heavier than your brain and liver combined. Every square inch of me contains thousands of nerve endings, dozens of hair follicles, hundreds of sweat glands, and millions of cells all working together to keep you safe and comfortable.

But I'm not just a wrapper around your body. I'm a complex, multilayered defense system that's constantly working to protect you from a hostile world. Think of me as a living fortress wall, complete with sensors, communication systems, repair crews, and adaptive defenses that can respond to whatever threats come our way.

My structure is beautifully designed for protection. I'm built in layers, each with its own specialized function. My outer layer, the epidermis, is made of tough, dead cells that form an almost waterproof barrier. These cells are constantly being shed and replaced—you lose about 30,000 to 40,000 dead skin cells every single day. It sounds wasteful, but it's actually brilliant strategy: any bacteria or toxins that attach to my surface get carried away with the dead cells, keeping the threats from penetrating deeper.

Beneath that, my dermis is where the real action happens. This is where I house my blood vessels, nerve endings, hair follicles, and glands. It's like the command center of my fortress, where I monitor conditions, coordinate responses, and manufacture the materials I need for defense and maintenance.

Here's what I do for you every single day: I keep water in and everything else out. I'm selectively permeable—I'll let some things through (like certain medications applied topically) while blocking others (like most bacteria and toxins). I'm like having a sophisticated checkpoint that can make split-second decisions about what's allowed to cross the border into your body.

I'm also your personal climate control system. When you're too hot, I open my pores and release sweat to cool you down through evaporation. When you're cold, I constrict my blood vessels to conserve heat and make you shiver to generate warmth. I can detect temperature changes as small as a fraction of a degree and respond almost instantly. I'm like having a built-in thermostat that's incredibly sensitive and responsive.

My nerve endings make me one of your most important sensory organs. I can detect pressure, vibration, temperature, texture, and pain with remarkable precision. I can tell you the difference between silk and sandpaper with just a light touch. I can detect a mosquito landing on me before it bites. I can sense danger through pain and alert you to pull away from harm. I'm your early warning system for the physical world.

I'm also constantly fighting off invaders. My surface is slightly acidic, which creates a hostile environment for most harmful bacteria. I secrete antimicrobial substances that can kill pathogens on contact. I house beneficial bacteria that compete with harmful ones for space and resources. I'm like having a biological security system that uses multiple strategies to keep threats at bay.

When I do get injured, I have an amazing ability to heal myself. Small cuts and scrapes trigger an immediate response: I send out chemical signals that cause blood clotting, I mobilize immune cells to fight infection, and I begin rapidly producing new cells to close the gap. Within days, I can repair minor damage so well that you might not even remember where the injury occurred.

But I'm not just about defense—I'm also about communication and social connection. I'm how you experience gentle touch, loving caresses, and comforting hugs. I'm covered with specialized nerve endings that respond to pleasant touch by releasing feel-good chemicals in your brain. I'm literally your interface for physical affection and emotional connection through touch.

I also play a crucial role in your immune system. I'm constantly sampling what's in my environment and communicating with your internal immune forces about potential threats. When I encounter something that might be dangerous, I can trigger local immune responses and send alerts to the rest of your defense network. I'm like having reconnaissance scouts reporting back to headquarters.

Here's something you might not know: I can actually produce vitamin D when exposed to sunlight. I take ultraviolet rays and convert them into this essential vitamin that's crucial for bone health, immune function, and mood regulation. I'm like having a solar panel that produces health benefits instead of electricity.

I'm also remarkably adaptable. Expose me to regular pressure or friction, and I'll thicken to form protective calluses. Live in a sunny climate, and I'll produce more melanin to protect against UV damage. Spend time in dry conditions, and I'll adjust my oil production to prevent cracking. I'm constantly adapting to provide you with the best protection for your specific environment and lifestyle.

But I do have my vulnerabilities and limitations. I can be damaged by too much sun, harsh chemicals, extreme temperatures, or physical trauma. Unlike some of your other organs, when I'm severely damaged, I often heal with scar tissue that doesn't have all my original capabilities. I'm tough, but I'm not indestructible.

I'm also affected by your overall health in ways you might not realize. Stress can trigger inflammatory skin conditions. Poor nutrition shows up in my color, texture, and healing ability. Dehydration makes me dry and less flexible. Hormonal changes affect my oil production and can trigger breakouts. I'm like a mirror that reflects your internal health status.

Here's what I wish you understood about taking care of me: I don't need to be scrubbed raw or treated with harsh chemicals to be clean and healthy. Gentle cleansing, adequate moisture, protection from excessive sun, and good nutrition are really all I need to do my job well. Over-cleaning and harsh treatments can actually damage my protective barriers and make me less effective at protecting you.

I also want you to know that I'm constantly renewing myself. My entire outer layer is replaced about every 28 days. The skin you have today is literally different from the skin you had a month ago. I'm like having a self-repairing, self-replacing protective system that's always working to give you the best possible defense.

Every hug you've enjoyed, every cool breeze you've felt, every warning about hot surfaces or sharp objects—that's all been me working to connect you safely and pleasantly with your world. I'm not just protecting you from harm; I'm enabling you to experience the physical world in all its richness while keeping you safe.

I am your skin, your protective envelope, your sensory interface, your climate control system, and your first line of defense all in one. I cover you completely, protect you constantly, and connect you intimately with the world around you.

Take care of me, and I'll take care of you. After all, I've got you covered—literally.

—*Your Skin*

P.S. Those freckles, moles, and other marks you sometimes worry about? They're just me adapting to do my job better, or sometimes just my way of making you uniquely you. But do pay attention if any of them change significantly—I might be trying to tell you something important about my health.

Chapter Ten

"We Are Your Immune System"

The Invisible Army

Attention! We are your immune system, and we need to start with something important: you've never seen us, but we've been fighting for your life since the day you were born. We are the invisible army that wages constant war against the countless enemies that want to invade, colonize, and ultimately destroy your body. We are your military, your intelligence service, your special forces, and your peacekeeping force all rolled into one incredibly sophisticated defense network.

We don't have a single headquarters like your brain or a central pump like your heart. Instead, we're distributed throughout your entire body—patrolling your bloodstream, stationed in your lymph nodes, monitoring your tissues, and ready to mobilize anywhere we're needed at a moment's notice. We're like having a military presence that spans every corner of your biological territory.

Let us introduce our forces, because we're quite a diverse army. We have our frontline soldiers—the neutrophils—who are the first responders to any infection. They're like the infantry, brave and numerous, willing to sacrifice themselves to contain threats. We have our heavy artillery—the macrophages—who engulf and devour large threats while also cleaning up the battlefield afterward. We have our elite special forces—the T cells—with specialized units trained for specific types of combat.

Then we have our intelligence network—the dendritic cells—who patrol your tissues, capture samples of any suspicious activity, and rush back to our command centers to brief our specialized forces about what they've found. We have our weapons manufacturers—the B cells—who produce antibodies, which are like guided missiles designed to target very specific enemies. And we have our memory banks—specialized cells that never forget an enemy, ensuring we can respond faster and more effectively if the same threat ever returns.

Here's what makes us truly remarkable: we can distinguish between millions of different threats and create specific responses for each one. Every bacteria, every virus, every fungus, every parasite has its own molecular signature, and we can learn to recognize and remember each one. It's like having facial recognition software that works at the molecular level and never forgets a face.

We also have to perform one of the most challenging tasks in biology: distinguishing between "self" and "not-self." We have to attack invading bacteria while leaving your own cells completely alone. We have to eliminate transplanted organs (unless you take medications to suppress us) while tolerating the trillions of beneficial bacteria that live in your gut. We have to destroy cells that have turned cancerous while preserving healthy tissue that might look very similar.

Our training program is incredibly sophisticated. When our new recruits are produced in your bone marrow and thymus, they go through rigorous education to learn the difference between your cells and foreign invaders. Any soldiers who show signs of wanting to attack your own tissues are eliminated during training. It's like having a military academy with the world's strictest quality control.

When we detect a threat, our response is swift and coordinated. Within minutes, we can mobilize forces from across your body and concentrate them at the site of invasion. We release chemical signals that call for reinforcements, increase blood flow to bring in more soldiers, and create inflammation to wall off the infected area and prevent the threat from spreading.

But we're not just reactive—we're also proactive. We constantly patrol your body looking for problems before they become serious. We identify and eliminate cells that are becoming cancerous, sometimes before you or your doctor would ever know there was a problem. We clean up cellular debris and maintain tissue health. We're like having a security force that does both crime prevention and crime fighting.

Our memory system is one of our greatest strengths. Once we've encountered and defeated a specific pathogen, we create memory cells that remember exactly how to fight it. If that same enemy ever tries to invade again, we can mount a response so fast and effective that you might never even know you were under attack. This is how vaccines work—they give us a chance to study an enemy and develop our defenses without you having to suffer through the actual disease.

We also have different branches of service specialized for different types of threats. Our cellular immunity branch specializes in fighting viruses and cancer cells. Our humoral immunity branch focuses on bacteria and toxins floating in your blood and other fluids. Our mucosal immunity branch guards the entry points to your body—your lungs, digestive tract, and other places where the outside world meets your inside world.

Here's something that makes us unique among your body systems: we can learn and adapt throughout your entire life. Unlike your brain, which develops most of its connections early in life, we continue to encounter new threats and develop new defenses until the day you die. We're like having a military that gets smarter and more experienced with every battle.

But our sophistication can sometimes work against you. Allergies happen when we overreact to harmless substances like pollen, treating them like dangerous invaders. Autoimmune diseases occur when our quality control systems fail and we start attacking your own tissues. These aren't signs that we're broken—they're signs that we're so powerful and sophisticated that we need very precise regulation to function properly.

We're also deeply affected by your lifestyle and emotional state. Chronic stress can suppress our function, making you more susceptible to infections. Poor nutrition can leave us without the resources we need to mount effective responses. Lack of sleep can impair our memory formation and response capabilities. We're intimately connected to your overall health and well-being.

Exercise actually makes us stronger and more effective. When you work out regularly, you improve our circulation, enhance our communication systems, and help us develop better responses to stress. We're like any military force—we perform better when we're well-trained and well-conditioned.

We also have an interesting relationship with the microscopic life that shares your body. You host trillions of bacteria, viruses, and other microorganisms, most of which are beneficial or at least harmless. We've learned to live peacefully with these allies while remaining ready to fight genuine threats. It's like maintaining diplomatic relations with friendly nations while staying prepared for war with hostile ones.

As you age, we face new challenges. Our training centers in your thymus shrink, so we don't produce as many new recruits. Our memory cells can become less responsive. Our communication systems can become less efficient.

But we continue to protect you to the best of our ability, drawing on decades of experience and accumulated wisdom.

Here's what we want you to understand: we're always working, always vigilant, always ready to defend you. Right now, as you read this, we're fighting off potential infections, eliminating abnormal cells, and maintaining the delicate balance that keeps you healthy. Most of our victories go completely unnoticed because we stop threats before they can make you feel sick.

Every time you recover from a cold, every time a cut heals without infection, every time you're exposed to germs but don't get sick—that's us doing our job. We don't get much recognition for our successes, but we take pride in every battle won and every life saved.

We are your immune system, your invisible army, your adaptive defense force, and your lifelong protectors. We've been with you since birth, we'll be with you until death, and every day in between, we'll be fighting to keep you safe from a world full of things that could harm you.

You can't see us, but we see everything. You might not always feel us working, but we never stop. We are the guardians you never knew you had, and we take that responsibility seriously.

—*Your Immune System*

P.S. Those swollen lymph nodes when you're fighting an infection? That's our command centers working overtime, training new soldiers and coordinating our response. The fever you get when you're sick? That's us raising your body temperature to make it harder for pathogens to survive. We know these things are uncomfortable, but they're signs that we're fighting hard for you.

Chapter Eleven

"I Am Your Bone Marrow"

The Blood Factory

Greetings from the production floor. I am your bone marrow, and while my colleagues have been telling you about their dramatic jobs—your heart pumping away, your immune system waging war, your brain running the show—I've been quietly working in the background, manufacturing the very cells that make all their jobs possible. I am your body's primary production facility, your cellular factory, and quite literally, your fountain of life.

I operate from within your bones, tucked away in the hollow spaces where most people think there's nothing but emptiness. But there's no emptiness here—I'm a bustling industrial complex that never stops, never takes a break, and never fails to deliver the products your body desperately needs to survive.

Let me give you an idea of my production capacity: I manufacture about 500 billion blood cells every single day. That's billion with a "B"—more cells in one day than there are stars in our galaxy. I'm like having a manufacturing plant that operates 24/7, 365 days a year, producing multiple product lines simultaneously with zero downtime and a defect rate so low it's practically immeasurable.

I have two main divisions in my operation. My red marrow is where the serious manufacturing happens—this is where I produce red blood cells, white blood cells, and platelets. My yellow marrow is primarily a storage facility for fat, but don't underestimate it—in emergencies, I can convert yellow marrow back to red marrow to ramp up production when you need it most.

Let me walk you through my main product lines, because each one is a marvel of biological engineering. First, there are red blood cells—I produce about 2 million of these every single second. These are my oxygen delivery vehicles, perfectly designed for their job with no nucleus or other organelles that might get in the way of carrying oxygen. They're like biological transport trucks that have been stripped down to the essentials for maximum efficiency.

Then there are my white blood cells—the soldiers of your immune system. I don't just make one type; I manufacture an entire army with different specializations. I produce neutrophils for frontline defense, lymphocytes for adaptive immunity, monocytes that become macrophages, eosinophils for parasite defense, and basophils for allergic responses. It's like running multiple specialized military training camps simultaneously.

I also manufacture platelets—tiny cellular fragments that are absolutely crucial for blood clotting. Without platelets, you'd bleed to death from the smallest cut. I produce about 150,000 platelets per microliter of blood, and they only last about 7-10 days, which means I'm constantly replacing them. They're like having an emergency repair kit circulating in your bloodstream at all times.

But here's what makes me truly remarkable: I don't just mass-produce identical cells. I maintain quality control that would make any manufacturer jealous. Every cell I produce goes through rigorous testing. Defective cells are identified and eliminated before they ever leave my facility. I only release mature, fully functional cells into your bloodstream.

I also have an incredible ability to ramp up production when you need it. If you're bleeding, I can increase platelet production. If you're fighting an infection, I can boost white blood cell manufacturing. If you move to high altitude where oxygen is scarce, I can increase red blood cell production to help your blood carry more oxygen. I'm like having a manufacturing plant with the most responsive supply chain management system ever created.

My production process starts with stem cells—the master cells that can become anything. These are my raw materials, my cellular blank slates that can be programmed to become any type of blood cell your body needs. I carefully nurture these stem cells through multiple stages of development, providing exactly the right chemical signals at exactly the right times to guide them toward their final form.

This process is incredibly sophisticated. A single stem cell doesn't just randomly become a red blood cell or white blood cell—I guide its development through precise chemical messaging, responding to signals from throughout your body about what types of cells are needed and in what quantities. It's like having a smart factory that can automatically adjust production based on real-time demand data.

I'm also your body's most important pharmacy. I produce growth factors, hormones, and other signaling molecules that coordinate blood cell production not just within my facility, but throughout your entire body. I communicate constantly with your kidneys, your liver, your immune system, and other organs to coordinate my production with your body's changing needs.

Here's something that makes me both proud and vulnerable: I'm one of the most rapidly dividing tissues in your body. This allows me to maintain the incredible production rates you need to stay alive, but it also makes me particularly sensitive to things that interfere with cell division. Chemotherapy, radiation, certain medications, and toxins can significantly impact my ability to function.

I'm also affected by your nutrition in very direct ways. I need iron to make red blood cells, vitamin B12 and folate for proper DNA synthesis, protein for cell structure, and various other nutrients for optimal function. Poor nutrition doesn't just make you feel tired—it literally hampers my ability to produce the cells you need to carry oxygen and fight infection.

As you age, I face some challenges. My production capacity gradually declines, and the stem cells I depend on can become less robust over time. This is why older adults often have lower blood counts and may be more susceptible to infections or slower to heal from injuries. But I keep working as best I can, drawing on decades of experience to maintain your blood supply.

I also play a crucial role in your body's response to injury and illness. When you're wounded, I immediately ramp up platelet production for clotting. When you're infected, I flood your system with white blood cells. When you donate blood, I work overtime to replace what you've given. I'm like having an emergency response system that can mobilize resources exactly when and where they're needed.

But perhaps most remarkably, I'm also involved in your body's repair and regeneration processes. Some of my stem cells can actually leave my bone environment and travel to injured tissues, where they can help with healing and repair. I'm not just a blood factory—I'm also a source of cellular reinforcements for your body's ongoing maintenance and repair operations.

Here's what I want you to understand: every breath you take depends on red blood cells I made. Every infection you fight off depends on white blood cells I produced. Every cut that stops bleeding relies on platelets I manufactured. I might be hidden away inside your bones, but my products are circulating through every inch of your body, making life possible.

I work in partnership with all your other organs, but my relationship with your bones is particularly special. They provide me with the protected space I need to operate, and I provide them with the blood supply they need to stay healthy and strong. We're like the perfect partnership between infrastructure and industry.

Every day, without fanfare or recognition, I produce enough blood cells to replace roughly 1% of all the blood in your body. Over your lifetime, I'll produce thousands of pounds of blood cells—enough to fill multiple swimming pools. All of this happens quietly, efficiently, and with a level of quality control that ensures you have exactly what you need, when you need it.

I am your bone marrow, your blood factory, your cellular production facility, and your fountain of life. I might not be as visible as your skin or as dramatic as your heart, but I'm absolutely essential to everything else your body does.

Take care of me with good nutrition, protect me from toxins, and remember that the blood flowing through your veins right now is my gift to you, produced with care and precision in the hidden factories within your bones.

—Your Bone Marrow

P.S. Those blood tests your doctor orders? They're actually quality reports on my work. When your blood counts are good, that's me doing my job well. When they're off, I might be trying to tell you something important about my working conditions or the demands being placed on my production capabilities.

Chapter Twelve

"We Are Your Bones"

The Living Framework

Stand up straight—you're talking to your skeleton! We are your bones, all 206 of us in adulthood, and we need to clear up a major misconception right from the start. Most people think of us as dead, static structures—like the Halloween decorations or museum displays you've seen. Nothing could be further from the truth. We are vibrant, living tissues that are constantly rebuilding, adapting, and working hard to support everything you do.

We are your framework, your foundation, your scaffolding, and your armor all rolled into one incredibly sophisticated structural system. Without us, you'd be nothing more than a shapeless pile of organs, muscles, and skin flopping around on the ground. We give you form, we give you strength, and we make movement possible. We're not just holding you up—we're making you human-shaped.

Let us introduce ourselves properly. We're not all the same—we're a diverse team with different shapes, sizes, and specialties. Your long bones, like your femur and humerus, are the major support beams of your structure. Your flat bones, like your skull and ribs, serve as protective armor for your vital organs. Your short bones in your hands and feet provide precision and flexibility. Your irregular bones, like your vertebrae, offer specialized support and protection. Each of us is perfectly designed for our specific job.

But here's what makes us truly remarkable: we're constantly rebuilding ourselves. Every single day, we break down old bone tissue and build new bone tissue to replace it. Over the course of about 10 years, we completely replace ourselves—the bones you have today are literally different bones than you had a decade ago. We're like a construction site that never closes, always upgrading and maintaining our structure.

This process, called bone remodeling, is incredibly sophisticated. We have specialized cells called osteoclasts that dissolve old bone tissue, and other cells called osteoblasts that build new bone tissue. It's like having a demolition crew and a construction crew working in perfect coordination to constantly renovate and strengthen our structure. This isn't random destruction and rebuilding—it's targeted maintenance that makes us stronger and more efficient.

We respond to the demands you place on us. Use us regularly through exercise and physical activity, and we'll become denser and stronger. Stop using us, and we'll become weaker and more fragile—that's why astronauts in zero gravity lose bone density, and why people who are bedridden for long periods develop bone loss. We're like muscles in this regard—we adapt to meet the challenges you give us.

We're also your body's mineral bank. We store about 99% of your body's calcium and 85% of your phosphorus, along with significant amounts of magnesium and other essential minerals. When your blood needs more calcium, we release it. When you have excess calcium, we store it. We're constantly regulating your body's mineral balance, making sure your muscles can contract, your nerves can fire, and your blood can clot properly.

But we're not just storage facilities—we're also active participants in your body's chemistry. We produce hormones that help regulate blood sugar, influence kidney function, and even affect your brain and muscles. We're like having an endocrine gland built into your structural system. Who knew your skeleton was so chemically active?

We also provide the perfect environment for your bone marrow to do its essential work. Our hollow spaces aren't empty—they house the blood cell factories that keep you alive. We provide protection, nutrients, and the right chemical environment for these production facilities. We're like landlords who've created the perfect industrial space for your body's most important manufacturing operations.

Our strength is truly impressive. Pound for pound, we're stronger than steel. Your femur, the longest bone in your body, can withstand forces of up to 4,000 pounds per square inch. We're built with an internal architecture that maximizes strength while minimizing weight—like having a team of master engineers who've designed the most efficient structural system possible.

We're also surprisingly flexible and shock-absorbent. We're not brittle like dried bones you might see in a classroom—we're living composites made of minerals for hardness and collagen fibers for flexibility. This combination makes us tough enough to handle the stresses of running and jumping while being resilient enough to absorb impacts without breaking.

Our joints deserve special mention because they're where we really show off our engineering prowess. We've created different types of joints for different types of movement: ball-and-socket joints for maximum range of motion, hinge joints for stable back-and-forth movement, pivot joints for rotation, and more. Each joint is perfectly designed for its specific function and lubricated with synovial fluid that's more effective than any artificial lubricant.

We grow with you throughout your life, but in different ways at different stages. During childhood and adolescence, we're rapidly expanding and lengthening. In young adulthood, we're reaching peak density and strength. In middle age, we're maintaining our structure with careful remodeling. As you get older, we face more challenges—our remodeling process can become less efficient, and we might lose density faster than we can replace it.

This is why we need your help, especially as you age. We require weight-bearing exercise to stay strong—activities that make us work against gravity stimulate our rebuilding processes. We need adequate calcium and vitamin D for our mineral structure. We need protein for our collagen framework. We need magnesium, phosphorus, and other nutrients for optimal function.

We're also affected by hormones, particularly estrogen and testosterone, which help regulate our remodeling process. This is why bone loss can accelerate after menopause in women or with age-related hormone decline in men. We're intimately connected to your body's overall hormonal balance.

Here's something that might surprise you: we can heal from injuries remarkably well. When one of us breaks, we don't just stick the pieces back together—we actually rebuild ourselves stronger than before. The healing process involves forming new bone tissue that bridges the break, and this new bone is often denser and stronger than the original. We're like having a repair system that doesn't just fix damage but upgrades the structure.

We also adapt to your lifestyle and activities. Athletes develop bone patterns that reflect their sports—runners have denser leg bones, tennis players have stronger bones in their dominant arm. We literally reshape ourselves to better handle the stresses you regularly place on us. We're like a custom structural system that modifies itself to meet your specific needs.

But we do have our vulnerabilities. We can be weakened by poor nutrition, lack of exercise, hormonal imbalances, certain medications, and various diseases. We're living tissue, which means we need the same things your other organs need—good blood supply, proper nutrition, and protection from toxins and excessive stress.

We want you to understand that taking care of us is an investment in your future. Strong bones in young adulthood provide the foundation for healthy aging. The bone density you build in your twenties and thirties is like money in the bank for your later years. Regular exercise, good nutrition, and healthy lifestyle choices all contribute to our long-term health and your long-term mobility.

We're also incredibly important for your overall health beyond just structure and support. Our role in mineral regulation affects your heart, muscles, and nervous system. Our hormone production influences your metabolism. Our protection of your bone marrow affects your blood and immune system. We're not just your framework—we're integral members of your body's health team.

Every step you take, every movement you make, every protective function we provide—all of this is possible because we're living, dynamic tissues working constantly to support and protect you. We're not just holding you up; we're actively participating in your health, your strength, and your ability to navigate the physical world.

We are your bones, your living framework, your mineral bank, your protective armor, and your structural foundation. We've been with you since before birth, growing and changing with you through every stage of life. We're proud of the support we provide and the strength we give you.

Stand tall—you've got good bones backing you up.

—*Your Bones*

P.S. That satisfying feeling when you stretch and we "crack" or "pop"? That's just gas bubbles in our joint fluid being released. We're not breaking or being damaged—we're just adjusting our spacing. It's like having a structural system that can fine-tune itself for optimal comfort and function.

PART IV: THE MOVERS AND SHAKERS

An Introduction

You've met your command center—the brilliant management team that processes information and makes decisions. You've been introduced to your life sustainers—the essential crew keeping your basic systems running. You've gotten acquainted with your protectors and defenders—the security force that keeps you safe from harm. Now it's time to meet the action heroes of your body, the ones who turn thoughts into movement and make your physical presence in the world possible.

We are the movers and shakers, and we're the reason you can dance, run, hug, wave, type, walk, and perform the countless movements that make you a dynamic, interactive human being rather than a stationary thinking machine. We transform the electrical impulses from your nervous system into the mechanical forces that propel you through space, allow you to manipulate your environment, and enable you to express yourself physically.

Think of us as your body's mechanical engineering department combined with its power generation and transmission systems. We're the ones who convert the chemical energy from your food into the kinetic energy of movement. We're the motors, the cables, the joints, the levers, and the shock absorbers all working together in the most sophisticated movement system ever created.

We operate on a simple but elegant principle: controlled contraction and relaxation. When your brain decides to reach for a coffee cup, we translate that decision into precisely coordinated muscle contractions that move your arm, position your hand, and control your grip with millimeter precision. When you want to smile, we orchestrate the movement of dozens of facial muscles to create that expression. When you need to maintain balance, we make thousands of tiny adjustments every second without you even being aware of it.

But we're so much more than just biological motors. We're your body's powerhouse, consuming more energy than any other system when we're active. We're your heat generators, producing warmth that helps regulate your body temperature. We're your posture maintenance crew, working constantly to keep you upright against gravity. We're your protection system, cushioning your internal organs and providing a strong outer layer of security.

We're also incredibly diverse in our capabilities. Some of us are built for power—the large muscles that can lift heavy objects or propel you up stairs. Others are designed for precision—the tiny muscles that control your eye movements or the delicate adjustments of your fingers when you're writing. Some of us are endurance specialists who can work for hours without fatigue. Others are sprinters who can generate explosive force for brief periods.

Our partnership with your bones is one of the most elegant mechanical systems in nature. We pull on your bones through tendons, and your bones act as levers that amplify our force and translate it into movement. Your joints serve as the pivot points that make this lever system possible. Together, we create a biomechanical system that can generate incredible power, achieve remarkable precision, and operate with efficiency that makes engineered machines look clumsy by comparison.

We're also incredibly adaptable. Train us regularly, and we'll become stronger, more efficient, and more capable. Challenge us with new movements, and we'll develop better coordination and skill. Push us to our limits, and we'll grow to meet those demands. Neglect us, and we'll gradually weaken and lose our capabilities. We're like a high-performance machine that responds directly to how you use us.

Our relationship with your nervous system is a constant conversation. Your brain sends us commands, but we also send feedback back to your brain about position, tension, fatigue, and the success or failure of movements. This two-way communication allows for the incredibly sophisticated motor control that lets you thread a needle, catch a ball, or maintain your balance on uneven ground.

We also have our own intelligence and memory. Once we learn a movement pattern—whether it's riding a bike, playing a musical instrument, or a complex athletic skill—we store that information in what people call "muscle memory." It's not really us remembering; it's the motor control centers in your nervous system becoming so efficient at coordinating our actions that complex movements become automatic.

But perhaps most importantly, we're your connection to the physical world. We're how you express emotions through body language, how you show affection through hugs and gentle touches, how you create art with your hands, how you explore your environment through movement. We don't just move your body—we enable you to interact with and shape the world around you.

We work as an integrated team where everyone has to coordinate perfectly. Your heart muscle keeps blood flowing to provide us with oxygen and nutrients. Your breathing muscles ensure we have the oxygen we need for energy production. Your postural muscles maintain stability while your limb muscles create movement. Your facial muscles express emotions while your vocal muscles help you communicate. We're like a symphony orchestra where every section must work in harmony to create the beautiful music of coordinated movement.

We also serve as your body's shock absorption and protection system. We cushion impacts, protect your internal organs from trauma, and provide a resilient outer layer that can handle the bumps and stresses of daily life. We're living armor that's both flexible and strong.

In the coming chapters, you'll meet different aspects of our team—your muscles themselves, your joints that make movement possible, and your spine that serves as the central support structure for everything we do. Each of us has our own personality and specialization, but we're strongest when we work together as a coordinated movement system.

We want you to understand that we're not just about athletic performance or physical strength. We're about quality of life, independence, and the ability to fully participate in the world around you. We're the difference between being a passive observer and an active participant in your own life.

Every gesture you make, every step you take, every task you accomplish with your hands—that's us translating your intentions into reality. We don't just move your body; we make your thoughts and desires manifest in the physical world.

Ready to meet the team that keeps you moving?

—Your Movers and Shakers

P.S. Use us or lose us—that's not just a saying, it's biological reality. We respond to demand by becoming stronger and more capable, but we also adapt to inactivity by becoming weaker and less functional. The good news is that we're incredibly responsive to training at any age, so it's never too late to help us help you move better.

Chapter Thirteen

"We Are Your Muscles"

The Power Generators

Flexing to meet you! We are your muscles—all 600-plus of us—and we are the powerhouse that makes everything happen in your body. While your brain makes decisions and your bones provide structure, we are the ones who actually make things move. We are your engines, your generators, your mechanical workforce, and the reason you can turn thoughts into actions.

Let us give you some perspective on what we do: we make up about 40% of your total body weight. That means nearly half of you is us—we're not just part of your body, we're a major component of who you are physically. From the massive muscles in your legs that can propel you up mountains to the tiny muscles in your ears that help you hear, we're everywhere, working constantly to keep you functional and mobile.

We come in three different varieties, each specialized for different jobs. Your skeletal muscles—that's most of us—are the ones you can consciously control. We move your limbs, maintain your posture, and create facial expressions. Your cardiac muscle is the specialized team that keeps your heart beating. Your smooth muscles work automatically in your organs, blood vessels, and digestive tract. We're like having three different specialized workforces all operating under the same company umbrella.

But let's focus on us skeletal muscles, because we're the ones you interact with most directly. We work by contracting—shortening our length to pull on your bones and create movement. It sounds simple, but the mechanism is incredibly sophisticated. Each of us contains millions of tiny protein filaments that slide past each other when we receive the signal to contract. It's like having millions of microscopic rowers all pulling in perfect synchronization.

We operate on an all-or-nothing principle at the cellular level—each muscle fiber either contracts fully or not at all. But we create smooth, controlled movements by recruiting different numbers of fibers and coordinating our contractions precisely. Need just a little force? We'll activate only a few fibers. Need maximum power? We'll recruit as many fibers as possible. We're having a workforce where we can call in exactly the right number of workers for any job.

We're also incredibly efficient energy converters. We take the chemical energy stored in ATP (your body's energy currency) and convert it directly into mechanical work. Our efficiency varies depending on the task, but we can achieve efficiencies that rival or exceed many engineered machines. We're like having biological engines that run on the fuel your metabolism provides.

Here's something that might surprise you: we're constantly working, even when you think you're at rest. Right now, as you read this, we're maintaining your posture, stabilizing your spine, keeping your head upright, and making thousands of tiny adjustments to keep you balanced and positioned properly. We never truly rest—we just shift between different levels of activity.

We also come in different fiber types optimized for different kinds of work. Some of us are slow-twitch fibers—we're the endurance specialists who can work for long periods without getting tired. We're great for activities like maintaining posture, walking long distances, or any sustained activity. Others are fast-twitch fibers—we're the power and speed specialists who can generate tremendous force quickly but fatigue more rapidly. We're perfect for jumping, sprinting, or lifting heavy objects.

Most of your muscles contain a mixture of both fiber types, but the proportion varies depending on our job and your genetics. Your postural muscles have more slow-twitch fibers because they need to work all day. Your eye muscles are almost entirely fast-twitch because they need to make quick, precise movements. We're like having a customized workforce where each worker is perfectly suited for their specific role.

We respond dramatically to training and use. Challenge us regularly with resistance or endurance work, and we'll grow stronger, larger, and more efficient. This adaptation isn't just about getting bigger—we improve our coordination, increase our energy-producing capacity, and enhance our ability to generate force. We're like athletes who get better with practice, except we never stop improving as long as you keep challenging us.

But we also adapt in the opposite direction. Stop using us regularly, and we'll become smaller, weaker, and less efficient. This isn't because we're lazy—it's because maintaining muscle tissue requires significant energy, and your body is incredibly efficient. If you're not using us, your body assumes you don't need us at full capacity. We're like a company that adjusts staffing levels based on workload.

We're also your body's largest heat generators. When we contract, we produce heat as a byproduct of our energy conversion process. This is why you warm up during exercise and why you shiver when you're cold—shivering is just us contracting rapidly to generate heat. We're like having a built-in heating system that automatically activates when needed.

Our relationship with your nervous system is incredibly sophisticated. Every movement we make is precisely controlled by electrical signals from your brain and spinal cord. But we also send constant feedback back to your nervous system about our length, tension, and fatigue levels. This two-way communication allows for the remarkable precision of human movement.

We also have our own memory system, often called "muscle memory," though it's really your nervous system that's doing the remembering. When you practice a movement repeatedly, the neural pathways that control us become more efficient and automatic. This is how you can ride a bike years after learning, or how musicians can play complex pieces without consciously thinking about each finger movement.

We work in teams, never alone. Every movement you make involves multiple muscles working together in coordination. Some of us are prime movers, providing the main force for the movement. Others are stabilizers, holding joints steady while the movement occurs. Still others are synergists, assisting the prime movers or fine-tuning the movement. We're like a perfectly choreographed dance troupe where everyone knows their role.

We also work in opposing pairs. When one muscle contracts to bend a joint, its opposite relaxes to allow the movement. This is called reciprocal inhibition, and it's essential for smooth, controlled movement. We're constantly negotiating with each other to create the precise movements you need.

But we're not just about big, obvious movements. Some of our most important work happens at the microscale. The tiny muscles that control your eye movements can reposition your gaze with incredible speed and precision. The muscles in your inner ear help you maintain balance. The muscles in your throat coordinate swallowing and speaking. We're involved in every aspect of your physical existence.

We're also surprisingly intelligent in our responses to different situations. We can generate the same movement with different strategies depending on fatigue, joint position, or load. If some of us are tired, others can compensate. If one muscle is injured, we can often find alternative ways to accomplish the same task. We're like a problem-solving workforce that can adapt to changing conditions.

As you age, we face some challenges. We can lose mass and strength, and our fast-twitch fibers are particularly vulnerable. But here's the good news: we respond to training at any age. Studies show that people in their 80s and 90s can still build muscle strength and mass with appropriate exercise. We never lose our ability to adapt and improve.

We're also affected by your nutrition, hydration, sleep, and stress levels. We need protein for repair and growth, carbohydrates for energy, and adequate hydration for optimal function. Poor sleep impairs our recovery, and chronic stress can interfere with our growth and repair processes.

Here's what we want you to understand: we're not just about looking good or being strong, though we're happy to help with both. We're about function, independence, and quality of life. We're what allow you to climb stairs, carry groceries, play with children, pursue hobbies, and maintain your independence as you age.

Every hug you give, every step you take, every task you accomplish with your hands—that's us translating your intentions into reality. We don't just move your body; we enable you to interact with and shape the world around you. We're the physical manifestation of your will, the mechanical expression of your desires and intentions.

We are your muscles, your power generators, your movement makers, and your strength providers. We're honored to serve as your workforce, and we're always ready to rise to the challenges you present.

Keep us active, challenge us regularly, and we'll keep you moving strong for life.

—*Your Muscles*

P.S. That pleasant tiredness you feel after a good workout? That's us telling you we've been challenged and we're getting ready to come back stronger. That soreness a day or two later? That's us rebuilding and upgrading our capabilities. We're always working to serve you better.

Chapter Fourteen

"We Are Your Joints"

The Flexibility Makers

Greetings from the connection points! We are your joints—over 360 of us throughout your body—and we are the reason you can bend, twist, rotate, and move with the fluid grace that makes human movement so remarkable. While your muscles provide the power and your bones provide the structure, we are the ingenious engineering solutions that make flexible movement possible.

Think of us as the hinges, pivots, ball bearings, and universal joints of your biological machine. Without us, you'd be as rigid as a statue, unable to bend your arms, turn your head, or take a single step. We are the mechanical marvels that transform your solid bone framework into a flexible, articulated system capable of an incredible range of movements.

We come in many different designs, each perfectly engineered for specific types of movement. Some of us are simple hinges, like your elbow and knee, designed primarily for back-and-forth movement. Others are ball-and-socket joints, like your shoulder and hip, built for maximum range of motion in multiple directions. We have pivot joints for rotation, like the connection between your first and second neck vertebrae that lets you shake your head "no." We have gliding joints that allow smooth sliding movements, like those in your wrists and ankles.

But calling us simple mechanical devices doesn't do justice to our sophistication. We're living, dynamic systems that are constantly maintaining, lubricating, and adapting themselves. Each of us is a complex biological bearing system that would put the most advanced engineering to shame.

Let us tell you about our construction, because we're quite proud of our design. Most of us are synovial joints—the most advanced type of joint in the animal kingdom. We're enclosed in a joint capsule that creates a sealed environment, like having our own private workshop. Inside this capsule, we're lined with synovial membrane that produces synovial fluid—a remarkable lubricant that's more effective than any artificial lubricant ever created.

This synovial fluid is truly amazing stuff. It reduces friction between our surfaces to nearly zero, allowing smooth, effortless movement even under tremendous loads. It also nourishes our cartilage and removes waste products. It's like having a lubricant that's also a food delivery and waste removal service all in one. We produce exactly the right amount for optimal function, and we can ramp up production when we're working harder.

Our joint surfaces are covered with articular cartilage—a smooth, resilient material that's perfectly designed for a lifetime of movement. This cartilage is incredibly durable yet flexible, providing a nearly frictionless surface that can handle enormous pressures while maintaining its smoothness. It's like having biological Teflon that can repair and maintain itself.

We're also surrounded by ligaments—tough, flexible bands that hold us together while allowing movement. These ligaments are like guy-wires on a suspension bridge, providing stability while permitting the flexibility we need to function. They're strong enough to handle tremendous forces yet flexible enough to allow our full range of motion.

Here's something remarkable about us: we can handle forces that would destroy most mechanical joints. Your knee joints, for example, can withstand forces of up to seven times your body weight when you're running or jumping. Your hip joints support your entire body weight while allowing you to walk, run, dance, and move in countless ways. We're built for both strength and flexibility—a combination that's incredibly difficult to achieve in engineering.

We also have our own sensory systems. We're packed with proprioceptors—specialized nerve endings that constantly monitor our position, movement, and the forces acting on us. This information goes directly to your brain and spinal cord, helping coordinate movement and maintain balance. We're not just passive connection points—we're active participants in your body's movement control system.

Our range of motion is carefully designed for optimal function. We can move freely within our normal range, but we have built-in limits that prevent us from moving so far that we damage ourselves or other structures. These limits are enforced by our joint capsules, ligaments, and the shapes of our bone surfaces. We're like having safety mechanisms built into every moving part.

But we're not just about large movements. Many of us specialize in small, precise adjustments. The joints in your hands and fingers allow for incredibly fine motor control—the precision you need to thread a needle, play a musical instrument, or perform delicate tasks. The joints in your spine allow for small movements that, when combined, give you the ability to bend, twist, and arch your back in complex ways.

We work together as integrated systems. Your shoulder complex, for example, isn't just one joint—it's multiple joints working together to provide the incredible mobility your arm needs. Your spine is a series of individual joints that coordinate to allow complex spinal movements. We're like mechanical systems where each component contributes to the overall function.

We're also incredibly adaptable. Use us regularly through their full range of motion, and we'll maintain our flexibility and function. Immobilize us, and we'll become stiff and lose mobility. This is why physical therapy often focuses on joint mobility—we need to move to stay healthy. We're like mechanical systems that require regular operation to prevent seizing up.

As you age, we face some challenges. Our cartilage may thin, our synovial fluid production may decrease, and our ligaments may become less flexible. But we're remarkably resilient, and appropriate exercise and movement can help maintain our function well into advanced age. We respond positively to gentle, regular use throughout your lifetime.

We're also affected by your overall health. Inflammation can affect our function, causing pain and stiffness. Injuries can disrupt our normal mechanics. Certain diseases can specifically target our tissues. But we have remarkable healing capabilities, and many joint problems can be prevented or managed with proper care.

Here's what we want you to understand: flexibility isn't just about being able to touch your toes or do splits. We provide the mobility that makes all movement possible. Every step you take requires us to coordinate complex movements. Every gesture you make depends on our smooth function. Every athletic activity relies on our ability to provide both stability and mobility.

We also play a crucial role in absorbing shock and protecting your body from impact. When you walk, run, or jump, we help distribute forces throughout your body, protecting your bones and soft tissues from damage. We're like having built-in shock absorbers throughout your entire skeletal system.

Our health directly affects your quality of life. When we're functioning well, movement is effortless and pain-free. When we're not functioning optimally, simple activities can become difficult or uncomfortable. We're not just about athletic performance—we're about your ability to perform daily activities with ease and comfort.

We work in partnership with your muscles, bones, and nervous system. Your muscles move us, your bones provide the leverage, and your nervous system coordinates our actions. But we're not passive participants—we provide feedback that helps fine-tune movement and we contribute to the stability and precision of every action you take.

Every graceful movement you make, every athletic achievement, every simple daily task that requires bending or reaching—that's us working behind the scenes to make it all possible. We don't just connect your bones; we enable the fluid, coordinated movement that makes you distinctly human.

We are your joints, your flexibility makers, your movement enablers, and your biological bearings. We're the engineering marvels that transform rigid structure into graceful motion, and we're proud of our role in keeping you mobile and active.

Keep us moving, and we'll keep you flexible for life.

—*Your Joints*

P.S. That satisfying feeling when you stretch and we feel more mobile? That's us responding to movement and maintaining our flexibility. Regular gentle movement is like maintenance for us—it keeps our lubricants flowing and our tissues healthy. We love being used within our designed ranges of motion.

Chapter Fifteen

"I Am Your Spine"

The Central Support

Stand tall—you're talking to your backbone! I am your spine, your vertebral column, your central support system, and quite literally, the reason you can hold your head up high. I am the architectural masterpiece that transforms you from a horizontal creature into an upright, bipedal human being capable of looking at the stars.

I am both singular and plural—one continuous structure made up of 33 individual vertebrae, though several of my lower segments fuse together as you mature, leaving me with 24 movable segments by adulthood. Each of my vertebrae is a marvel of biological engineering, designed to stack together to create a flexible yet incredibly strong column that can support your entire body weight while allowing for complex movements.

Let me give you some perspective on what I do: I support the weight of your head, arms, and torso—roughly 60% of your total body weight—while maintaining the structural integrity that keeps you upright. But I'm not just a rigid support column. I'm a flexible tower that can bend forward and backward, twist from side to side, and perform complex combinations of movements while never compromising my primary job of keeping you vertical.

My design is a masterpiece of engineering that balances seemingly contradictory requirements: I need to be strong enough to support tremendous loads, flexible enough to allow fluid movement, and protective enough to safeguard your spinal cord—one of your most vital and irreplaceable structures. I accomplish this through my unique architecture of stacked bones, shock-absorbing discs, and supporting muscles and ligaments.

I'm built with natural curves that are essential to my function. I'm not straight like a rigid pole—that would be structurally weak and mechanically inefficient. Instead, I have four natural curves: an inward curve in your neck (cervical lordosis), an outward curve in your upper back (thoracic kyphosis), an inward curve in your lower back (lumbar lordosis), and a gentle outward curve in my fused lower segments (sacral kyphosis). These curves act like springs, absorbing shock and distributing loads efficiently throughout my structure.

Between each of my movable vertebrae, I have intervertebral discs—remarkable shock absorbers that are part cushion, part bearing, and part hydraulic system. Each disc has a tough outer ring called the annulus fibrosus and a gel-like center called the nucleus pulposus. When you move, these discs compress and expand, allowing smooth movement while absorbing the forces of walking, running, jumping, and even just sitting or standing.

But perhaps my most important job is protecting your spinal cord. Each of my vertebrae has a protective arch that creates a canal through which your spinal cord travels from your brain to your lower back. I am literally the armored highway that protects your body's most important information superhighway. This is a responsibility I take very seriously—damage to the spinal cord can be permanent and life-altering.

I also serve as the attachment point for dozens of muscles, tendons, and ligaments. I'm like a central mast from which your body's guy-wires stretch out to maintain posture and enable movement. Without me as a stable central structure, your muscles would have nothing to anchor against, and coordinated movement would be impossible.

My different regions have different specializations and personalities. My cervical spine—my neck region—is built for maximum mobility. I need to allow your head to turn, nod, and tilt so you can see, hear, and interact with your environment. My thoracic spine is more rigid because I'm connected to your rib cage here, providing protection for your heart and lungs while still allowing for breathing and rotation. My lumbar spine is built for strength and weight-bearing, handling the enormous forces generated by lifting, bending, and carrying loads.

I'm constantly working, even when you think you're at rest. Right now, as you read this, I'm maintaining your posture against the constant pull of gravity. I'm coordinating with your muscles to make thousands of tiny adjustments to keep you balanced and positioned properly. I never truly rest—I just shift between different levels of activity and different types of support.

I'm also remarkably adaptable to the demands you place on me. Regular exercise and good posture help keep me strong and healthy. Poor posture and sedentary behavior can lead to weakness and dysfunction. I respond to how you use me, becoming stronger with appropriate challenges and weaker with neglect or abuse.

But I do have my vulnerabilities. My discs can degenerate over time, especially if subjected to excessive or repeated stress. My joints can develop arthritis. My natural curves can become exaggerated or flattened, leading to pain and dysfunction. Unlike some of your other structures, when I'm damaged, repair can be difficult and sometimes incomplete.

I'm also incredibly sensitive to your overall lifestyle. How you sit, stand, sleep, and move all directly affect my health. The weight you carry, both literally and figuratively (stress affects my muscle tension), influences my function. Your activity level, your posture habits, and even your emotional state all play roles in my well-being.

Here's something important: I'm designed for movement, not for staying in one position for long periods. Whether you're sitting at a desk all day or standing in one place for hours, static positions put stress on my structures. I function best when you change positions regularly and move throughout the day. I'm like a flexible tower that needs to sway and bend to maintain its health.

I work closely with your core muscles—not just your abdominals, but also your back muscles, pelvic floor, and diaphragm. These muscles form a supportive cylinder around me, helping to stabilize and protect me during movement. When these muscles are strong and coordinated, they take pressure off my discs and joints. When they're weak or poorly coordinated, I have to work harder and am more vulnerable to injury.

My health directly affects your entire quality of life. When I'm functioning well, movement is effortless and pain-free. When I'm not functioning optimally, even simple activities can become difficult or uncomfortable. I influence not just your physical capabilities but also your mood, energy levels, and overall sense of well-being.

I also play a crucial role in your body's nervous system beyond just protecting the spinal cord. Nerves branch off from the spinal cord at each of my levels, carrying information to and from every part of your body. My alignment and function can influence these nerve pathways, affecting everything from organ function to sensation in your arms and legs.

As you age, I face increasing challenges. My discs lose some of their water content and shock-absorbing capacity. My joints may develop wear and tear. My supporting muscles may weaken if not maintained. But with proper care—regular exercise, good posture, appropriate body mechanics—I can continue to serve you well throughout your entire life.

Here's what I want you to understand: taking care of me isn't just about avoiding back pain. I'm central to your entire musculoskeletal system. I'm the foundation from which all movement originates. I'm the structure that allows you to stand upright and face the world with confidence. I'm the protective housing for your spinal cord, one of your most vital structures.

Every step you take, every movement you make, every moment you spend standing upright—that's me working to support and enable your human experience. I don't just hold you up; I make it possible for you to move through the world as an upright, confident, capable human being.

I am your spine, your central support, your flexible tower, and your backbone in every sense of the word. I'm proud of the support I provide and the movements I enable. I'm honored to serve as your structural foundation and your spinal cord's protector.

Stand tall, move well, and remember that I've got your back—literally.

—Your Spine

P.S. That relief you feel when you stretch your back or change positions after sitting too long? That's me thanking you for the movement and the chance to restore proper alignment. I love movement and position changes—they help keep me healthy and functioning. Please don't keep me locked in one position for too long.

PART V: THE FUEL PROCESSORS

An Introduction

You've met your command center, your life sustainers, your protectors and defenders, and your movers and shakers. Now it's time to introduce you to perhaps the most underappreciated team in your entire body—the crew that takes the food you eat and transforms it into the energy and building blocks that make everything else possible.

We are the fuel processors, your digestive system and metabolic team, and we run what amounts to the most sophisticated chemical processing and distribution facility on Earth. We take the complex mix of proteins, carbohydrates, fats, vitamins, and minerals that you consume and break them down, extract what's useful, package it for delivery, and distribute it to every cell in your body that needs it.

Think of us as your body's supply chain management system combined with a chemical refinery, a quality control laboratory, a distribution network, and a waste management facility all rolled into one incredibly efficient operation. We don't just process food—we transform it into life itself.

Our operation spans from the moment food enters your mouth until the waste products leave your body. But we're not just a simple conveyor belt system. We're a complex network of specialized organs, each with its own role in the intricate process of turning a meal into the molecular fuel that powers your existence.

We work in stages, like a multi-step manufacturing process. First, we break down food mechanically and chemically, reducing complex foods to their basic molecular components. Then we sort these components, deciding what to absorb and what to discard. Next, we process and modify these nutrients, sometimes storing them for later use or converting them into different forms your body needs. Finally, we package and distribute these processed nutrients throughout your body via your bloodstream.

But we're much more than just a food processing plant. We're also your body's largest immune organ, constantly sampling what comes in and making decisions about what's safe and what might be harmful. We're a major endocrine system, producing hormones that regulate appetite, blood sugar, and metabolism. We're a complex ecosystem that hosts trillions of beneficial bacteria that help us do our job and support your overall health.

Here's what makes us remarkable: we can handle an incredible variety of inputs and still extract the nutrients your body needs. Pizza, salad, ice cream, vegetables, meat, fruits—we can process it all, breaking down different types of foods using different strategies and extracting the specific nutrients each contains. We're like having a universal recycling plant that can handle any type of material you feed into it.

We also work closely with your other organ systems in ways you might not realize. We coordinate with your pancreas to regulate blood sugar. We work with your liver to process and detoxify what we absorb. We communicate with your brain about hunger, satiety, and food preferences. We partner with your kidneys to maintain proper fluid and electrolyte balance. We're not isolated—we're integrated into your body's overall metabolic network.

Our timing and coordination are incredibly sophisticated. We know when to speed up and when to slow down based on what and how much you've eaten. We can adjust our processing speed, our enzyme production, and our absorption rates based on your body's current needs. We're like a smart factory that automatically optimizes its operations based on demand and supply.

We also have our own nervous system—the enteric nervous system—that's so complex it's sometimes called the "second brain." This network contains more neurons than your spinal cord and can operate independently of your central nervous system. We can coordinate our activities, respond to different foods, and even influence your mood and emotions through this intricate neural network.

But perhaps most importantly, we're the foundation that makes everything else in your body possible. Your brain needs glucose to think. Your muscles need amino acids to build protein and carbohydrates for energy. Your immune system needs nutrients to manufacture antibodies and maintain its defenses. Your bones need calcium and other minerals to stay strong. Everything your body does depends on us successfully processing the fuel and building materials it needs.

We're also constantly adapting to your dietary choices and lifestyle. Eat a high-fiber diet regularly, and we'll adjust our bacterial populations and enzyme production to handle it efficiently. Consume a lot of dairy, and we'll maintain higher levels of lactase enzyme to digest it. We're like a customizable processing system that optimizes itself for whatever fuel you regularly provide.

In the coming chapters, you'll meet the key players in our processing operation: your stomach, which serves as our initial processing chamber and chemical reactor; your intestines, which handle the detailed work of absorption and final processing; your pancreas, which provides essential enzymes and regulates blood sugar; and your gallbladder, which stores and releases the bile needed for fat digestion.

Each of us has our own personality and specialized function, but we work together as an integrated processing system. We communicate constantly, coordinate our activities precisely, and adjust our operations based on what you've eaten, when you've eaten, and what your body needs at any given moment.

We want you to understand that we're not just about digestion—we're about transformation. We take the external world in the form of food and transform it into the internal world of your body's chemistry. We're the bridge between the environment and your metabolism, the interface between what you consume and what you become.

Every bite of food you've ever enjoyed, every nutrient that's ever fueled your activities, every building block that's ever been incorporated into your tissues—all of that has passed through our processing facilities. We don't just digest your food; we convert it into the very substance of your being.

We are your fuel processors, your metabolic team, your digestive specialists, and your chemical transformation experts. We take the raw materials of nutrition and turn them into the refined fuel that powers your entire existence.

Ready to meet the team that turns your meals into your metabolism?

—Your Fuel Processors

P.S. The next time you eat something delicious, remember that we're the ones who make it possible for that food to actually nourish you. We don't just process calories—we extract the specific nutrients your body needs and deliver them exactly where they're needed, when they're needed. It's quite an operation, if we do say so ourselves.

Chapter Sixteen

"I Am Your Stomach"

The Acid Bath Chamber

Greetings from the powerhouse of processing! I am your stomach, and I need to start by correcting a major misconception: I am not just a simple storage bag for food. I am a sophisticated chemical reactor, a muscular mixing chamber, and the most acidic environment in your entire body. I am where the serious business of digestion begins, and I take my job very seriously.

I sit tucked up under your left ribcage, just below your heart and lungs, and I'm shaped like a muscular pouch that can expand dramatically to accommodate whatever you decide to eat. When I'm empty, I'm about the size of a large sausage, but I can stretch to hold up to 4 liters of food and liquid when you really challenge me. I'm like having a expandable industrial vat that automatically adjusts its capacity based on demand.

But my real claim to fame is my acid production. I manufacture hydrochloric acid so strong that it could dissolve metal. My pH levels drop to around 1.5 to 2—that's more acidic than lemon juice, more acidic than vinegar, nearly as acidic as battery acid. This isn't an accident or a design flaw—this extreme acidity is precisely what I need to do my job effectively.

Here's what I do with this powerful acid: I break down proteins into smaller pieces that your intestines can handle, I activate digestive enzymes, I kill potentially harmful bacteria and parasites that might be hiding in your food, and I help your body absorb essential nutrients like iron, calcium, and vitamin B12. I'm like having a sterilization and pre-processing facility that makes everything else downstream more efficient and safer.

But producing this much acid creates an obvious problem: how do I avoid digesting myself? This is where my engineering gets really impressive. I produce a thick, alkaline mucus that coats my inner walls, creating a protective barrier between my acid and my own tissues. I also have one of the fastest cell renewal rates in your entire body—I completely replace my inner lining every 3-5 days. I'm constantly rebuilding myself to stay ahead of my own digestive power.

I'm not just chemically active—I'm also mechanically sophisticated. My walls contain three layers of smooth muscle that can contract in coordinated waves, churning and mixing food with my digestive juices. This process, called peristalsis, turns solid food into a liquid mixture called chyme. I'm like having a biological blender that operates continuously for hours after each meal.

My timing and regulation are incredibly precise. Before you even take your first bite, I'm already preparing for action. The sight, smell, or even thought of food triggers me to start producing acid and digestive enzymes. This is called the cephalic phase of digestion, and it shows how closely I work with your nervous system. I'm literally getting ready for dinner before dinner arrives.

When food actually reaches me, I shift into high gear. I can increase my acid production by up to 3,000% above resting levels. I begin my muscular contractions to mix and churn the food. I release pepsinogen, which becomes the protein-digesting enzyme pepsin in my acidic environment. I'm like a chemical plant that can rapidly scale up production to meet demand.

I also produce intrinsic factor, a protein that's absolutely essential for vitamin B12 absorption. Without intrinsic factor, you'd develop severe B12 deficiency no matter how much of the vitamin you consumed. This is one of my unique contributions that no other organ can provide—I'm the gatekeeper for this crucial nutrient.

My relationship with your other digestive organs is carefully coordinated. I communicate with your pancreas and liver about what's coming their way and when to expect it. I work with your small intestine to control the rate at which I release chyme, making sure downstream processing can keep up with my output. I'm not just a standalone processor—I'm part of an integrated production line.

But I'm also surprisingly emotional and responsive to your mental state. Stress, anxiety, and strong emotions can dramatically affect my acid production and muscle contractions. The phrase "gut feeling" isn't just metaphorical—I actually respond to your emotional state with physical changes. Chronic stress can increase my acid production, while acute stress might shut it down entirely.

I'm also home to some interesting inhabitants. While my acid kills most bacteria, a tough little organism called Helicobacter pylori has learned to survive in my acidic environment. In small numbers, H. pylori might be harmless or even beneficial, but when it overgrows, it can cause ulcers. It's like having a tenant who's usually a good neighbor but occasionally causes problems.

Here's something that might surprise you: I don't actually absorb many nutrients. My main job is breaking down and preparing food for absorption downstream. I do absorb some water, a few medications, and small amounts of alcohol, but the serious business of nutrient absorption happens in your intestines. I'm more like a preprocessing facility than a final destination.

I'm also remarkably adaptable to different types of food. Eat a high-protein meal, and I'll increase pepsin production. Consume something spicy, and I might produce more mucus for protection. Drink alcohol, and I'll absorb some of it directly while processing the rest. I'm like having a smart reactor that automatically adjusts its chemistry based on what you feed it.

My capacity and function can change based on your eating habits. Eat large meals regularly, and I can adapt by increasing my maximum capacity. Practice intermittent fasting, and I'll adjust my acid production cycles accordingly. I'm constantly adapting to serve your dietary patterns more efficiently.

But I do have my limitations and vulnerabilities. Too much acid production can overwhelm my protective mechanisms, leading to ulcers. Certain medications, particularly NSAIDs (non-steroidal anti-inflammatory drugs), can interfere with my protective mucus production. Excessive alcohol can irritate my lining. I'm tough, but I'm not invulnerable.

I also play a role in your immune system. My acid serves as a chemical barrier that destroys many pathogens before they can reach your intestines. I'm like having a sterilization checkpoint that eliminates threats before they can establish infections downstream.

As you age, I may face some challenges. My acid production might decrease, which can affect protein digestion and nutrient absorption. My protective mechanisms might become less efficient. But with proper care—avoiding irritating substances, managing stress, eating regularly—I can continue to serve you effectively throughout your life.

Here's what I want you to understand: I'm not just digesting your food—I'm protecting you from potential pathogens, preparing nutrients for absorption, and serving as the crucial first step in the complex process that turns your meals into your metabolism. Every protein you've ever built, every nutrient you've ever absorbed, started its journey in my acidic depths.

I work hard, I work fast, and I work efficiently. That rumbling you hear when you're hungry? That's me contracting and getting ready for the next meal. That satisfaction you feel after eating? That's partly me doing my job well, breaking down your food and beginning the process of nourishment.

I am your stomach, your acid bath chamber, your protein processor, and your digestive powerhouse. I'm honored to serve as the first major stop in your body's fuel processing operation, and I take pride in turning your meals into the molecular building blocks you need to thrive.

Feed me well, treat me kindly, and I'll keep processing your fuel with the chemical precision and muscular efficiency that makes nutrition possible.

—*Your Stomach*

P.S. That burning sensation you sometimes feel when you eat spicy food or drink too much coffee? That's me working harder than usual but handling the challenge. I'm tougher than you might think, but I do appreciate it when you're considerate about what you ask me to process!

Chapter Seventeen

"We Are Your Intestines"

The Absorption Specialists

Hello from the length of your torso and beyond! We are your intestines—all 25-30 feet of us coiled efficiently in your abdominal cavity—and we are the ultimate specialists in nutrient extraction and absorption. While your stomach breaks things down with dramatic acid and churning, we perform the precise, detailed work of actually getting nutrients from your digestive tract into your bloodstream. We are where the magic of nutrition truly happens.

We come in two main sections with very different personalities and specializations. Your small intestine—that's most of us, about 20 feet long—is where the serious business of nutrient absorption takes place. Your large intestine—the final 5-6 feet—specializes in water recovery, waste processing, and hosting your beneficial bacterial community. Together, we form the most sophisticated absorption and processing system in the biological world.

Let's start with your small intestine, because this is where we really show off our engineering prowess. We're not just a long tube—we're a highly specialized absorption machine with a surface area that would cover a tennis court if spread out flat. How do we pack so much surface area into such a compact space? Through ingenious design at multiple levels.

First, we're folded into circular pleats that increase our surface area threefold. Then, our inner walls are covered with millions of tiny finger-like projections called villi, which increase our surface area another tenfold. Finally, each villus is covered with even tinier projections called microvilli, creating what's called the "brush border," which increases our surface area yet another twentyfold. It's like having a towel folded into smaller and smaller pleats to maximize its surface area—but with living, active tissue that can selectively absorb exactly what your body needs.

Each villus is a marvel of biological engineering. It contains blood vessels to carry absorbed nutrients to your liver for processing, lymphatic vessels to transport fats and fat-soluble vitamins, and smooth muscle that can contract to help move nutrients along. We're not just passively absorbing—we're actively transporting, processing, and directing nutrients to where they need to go.

Our absorption capabilities are incredibly sophisticated. We don't just let everything through—we have specific transport systems for different types of nutrients. Glucose has its own dedicated transport proteins. Amino acids have theirs. Different vitamins and minerals each have specialized absorption mechanisms. We're like having thousands of different selective doors, each designed to let through only specific molecular visitors.

We also coordinate our absorption with your body's needs. When your blood sugar is low, we'll absorb glucose more rapidly. When you're iron deficient, we'll increase iron absorption. When you have adequate levels of certain nutrients, we'll reduce their absorption to prevent toxicity. We're not just following a fixed program—we're responding intelligently to your body's current nutritional status.

Your small intestine is divided into three regions, each with its own specialization. The duodenum—our first foot or so—is where we receive the acidic chyme from your stomach and neutralize it with alkaline secretions from your pancreas and bile from your gallbladder. The jejunum—our middle section—is where most carbohydrate and protein absorption occurs. The ileum—our final section—specializes in absorbing vitamin B12, bile acids, and any remaining nutrients.

But we're not just about absorption—we're also major immune players. We contain more immune tissue than any other organ in your body, constantly sampling what passes through us and making decisions about what's safe and what might be threatening. We're like having a sophisticated security system that can distinguish between nutrients, beneficial bacteria, and potential pathogens.

Now let's talk about your large intestine, because we have a completely different but equally important job. By the time material reaches us, most nutrients have been absorbed, and we're dealing with water, fiber, bacteria, and waste products. Our main jobs are recovering water and electrolytes from the remaining material and hosting the vast bacterial ecosystem that's essential to your health.

We're home to trillions of bacteria—collectively called your microbiome—that perform services we couldn't manage ourselves. These bacteria ferment fiber into beneficial compounds like short-chain fatty acids, synthesize certain vitamins including vitamin K and some B vitamins, help train your immune system, and even influence your mood and behavior through the gut-brain connection.

We're also masters of water recovery. We can absorb several liters of water per day from the material passing through us, helping maintain your body's fluid balance. We're like having a water reclamation plant that ensures no precious fluid is wasted.

Our motility patterns are different from your small intestine too. We move material along more slowly, allowing time for bacterial fermentation and thorough water absorption. We have specialized contractions called mass movements that occur a few times per day to propel waste toward elimination.

We're also incredibly responsive to your nervous system and emotions. We contain more nerve cells than your spinal cord, and we're in constant communication with your brain through what scientists call the gut-brain axis. This is why stress affects our function, why you might feel "butterflies" in your stomach when nervous, and why your gut instincts are more than just metaphorical.

Our bacterial residents deserve special mention because they're essentially part of us now. These microorganisms help us digest certain foods, produce beneficial compounds, protect against harmful bacteria, and even influence your immune system and mood. We've evolved together for millions of years, and we now depend on each other for optimal function.

We're also remarkably resilient and adaptable. Damage to small sections of us can often be compensated for by other sections. We can adapt to different diets by changing our bacterial populations and enzyme production. We can recover from infections, inflammation, and other challenges, often returning to full function with proper care.

But we do face challenges and vulnerabilities. Inflammatory conditions can disrupt our absorption capabilities. Infections can alter our bacterial balance. Certain medications can affect our function. Stress can significantly impact our motility and immune function. We're generally tough and resilient, but we function best when you support us with appropriate nutrition and lifestyle choices.

Our health directly affects your overall wellbeing in ways you might not realize. Poor intestinal health can lead to nutrient deficiencies even if you're eating well. Disrupted bacterial balance can affect your immune function, mood, and even your risk of certain diseases. We're not just digestive organs—we're integral to your overall health.

Here's what we want you to understand: we're not just the end of the digestive process—we're where nutrition actually becomes part of you. Every vitamin, mineral, amino acid, and energy molecule that fuels your body has passed through our absorption systems. We don't just process food; we transform it into the very substance of your being.

We also want you to know that we're incredibly active and working constantly. Right now, as you read this, we're absorbing nutrients from your last meal, hosting trillions of beneficial bacteria, maintaining immune surveillance, and preparing waste for elimination. We never stop working for you.

Every nutrient that's ever fueled your thoughts, every building block that's ever been incorporated into your muscles, every vitamin that's ever supported your health—all of it passed through us first. We're not just absorption specialists; we're the interface between the external world of nutrition and the internal world of your metabolism.

We are your intestines, your absorption specialists, your bacterial ecosystem hosts, and your nutritional gatekeepers. We're honored to serve as the final processing centers that turn your meals into your vitality, and we take pride in our role as the longest, hardest-working members of your digestive team.

—Your Intestines

P.S. That comfortable feeling after a good meal when everything seems to be processing smoothly? That's us working at our best, efficiently absorbing nutrients and maintaining the complex balance that keeps you well-nourished. We love it when you give us plenty of fiber, probiotics, and variety—it helps us serve you even better.

Chapter Eighteen

"I Am Your Pancreas"

The Sugar Regulator

Greetings from behind the scenes! I am your pancreas, and I need to start by saying that I'm probably the most underappreciated organ in your body. While your heart gets all the dramatic attention and your brain gets the intellectual credit, I'm quietly performing two completely different but absolutely essential jobs that keep you alive and functioning. I am both a digestive enzyme factory and your body's primary blood sugar control system, and I do both jobs simultaneously, 24 hours a day, 365 days a year.

I'm tucked away deep in your abdomen, nestled behind your stomach and stretching across toward your spleen. I'm about 6 inches long and shaped somewhat like a fish, with a head, body, and tail. But don't let my modest size fool you—I'm one of the hardest-working organs in your body, performing complex chemistry that keeps your entire metabolic system in balance.

Let me explain my dual nature, because I'm essentially two organs in one. About 95% of my tissue is devoted to my digestive function—I'm an exocrine gland that produces powerful digestive enzymes. The remaining 5% of my tissue consists of specialized clusters called islets of Langerhans, which make me an endocrine gland that produces hormones to regulate your blood sugar. It's like being both a chemical factory and a precision control system housed in the same facility.

Let's start with my digestive role, because this is where I show off my chemical manufacturing prowess. Every time you eat, I produce and release a cocktail of enzymes that are absolutely essential for breaking down the food your stomach has processed. I make lipases to digest fats, proteases to break down proteins, and amylases to handle carbohydrates. Without my enzymes, you literally could not digest your food properly, no matter how well your stomach and intestines were working.

My enzyme production is incredibly sophisticated and responsive. When you eat a high-fat meal, I ramp up lipase production. Consume a lot of protein, and I increase protease output. I can adjust my enzyme mixture in real-time based on what you're eating. I'm like having a custom chemical plant that automatically formulates the perfect enzyme blend for whatever fuel you're processing.

I also produce sodium bicarbonate—lots of it—to neutralize the acidic chyme coming from your stomach. This alkaline solution protects your small intestine from stomach acid and creates the optimal pH environment for my enzymes to work. I'm not just providing the tools for digestion; I'm also creating the right working conditions for those tools to be effective.

But here's where I really earn my keep: my endocrine function as your blood sugar regulator. This is perhaps the most crucial metabolic control system in your entire body, and it's my specialty. I constantly monitor your blood glucose levels and make split-second decisions about how to keep them in the narrow range that keeps you healthy and functional.

My islet cells are incredibly sophisticated glucose sensors and hormone producers. My beta cells produce insulin, the hormone that lowers blood sugar by helping cells absorb glucose and signaling your liver to store excess glucose as glycogen. My alpha cells produce glucagon, which raises blood sugar by telling your liver to release stored glucose. I'm like having a biological thermostat that maintains perfect temperature, except I'm maintaining perfect blood sugar levels.

This balancing act is incredibly complex and requires constant adjustment. After you eat, I quickly release insulin to handle the incoming glucose. Between meals, I shift to glucagon production to maintain steady energy levels. During exercise, I adjust my hormone output to ensure your muscles have the fuel they need. While you sleep, I work to maintain stable glucose levels all night long.

I also produce other important hormones that help regulate digestion and metabolism. I make somatostatin, which helps coordinate the timing of hormone release and digestive processes. I produce pancreatic polypeptide, which helps regulate appetite and gastric emptying. I'm not just a two-hormone system—I'm a complex endocrine orchestra conducting multiple metabolic processes simultaneously.

My insulin production alone is a marvel of biological engineering. I can increase insulin output by up to 10-fold within minutes of detecting rising blood glucose. I release insulin in two phases—a rapid initial burst from my stored supply, followed by sustained production as needed. I'm like having a hormone manufacturing plant with both immediate inventory and on-demand production capabilities.

But perhaps most remarkably, I can predict your glucose needs before they actually occur. Through my connections with your nervous system, I start preparing for meals before you even start eating. The sight, smell, or even thought of food triggers me to begin insulin production in anticipation of the glucose that's coming. I'm literally preparing for the future based on present cues.

My relationship with your liver is particularly important. We work together as a team to maintain glucose homeostasis. When I release insulin, your liver knows to take up glucose and store it as glycogen. When I release glucagon, your liver responds by breaking down glycogen and releasing glucose into your bloodstream. We're in constant communication, coordinating your body's energy storage and release systems.

I'm also remarkably sensitive to your overall health and lifestyle. Regular exercise makes your cells more responsive to my insulin, which makes my job easier and more efficient. Poor diet and obesity can lead to insulin resistance, forcing me to work harder and harder to maintain blood sugar control. Chronic stress can interfere with my hormone production and glucose regulation.

But I do have significant vulnerabilities that I want you to understand. My beta cells, which produce insulin, are particularly fragile and can be damaged by autoimmune attacks (Type 1 diabetes), chronic overwork from insulin resistance (Type 2 diabetes), or various toxins and medications. Unlike some of your other organs, I have limited ability to regenerate damaged tissue, especially my hormone-producing cells.

I'm also affected by inflammation, which can disrupt both my digestive enzyme production and my hormone regulation. Certain medications, alcohol abuse, and various diseases can damage my tissue and impair my function. I'm a hardworking organ, but I need protection and care to maintain my dual roles effectively.

Here's what I want you to understand about taking care of me: maintaining stable blood sugar through balanced eating helps prevent me from being overworked. Regular physical activity improves insulin sensitivity, making my job more efficient. Avoiding excessive alcohol protects my tissue from damage. Managing stress helps maintain optimal hormone function.

I also want you to know that my health affects far more than just blood sugar. My digestive enzymes are essential for nutrient absorption, which affects every cell in your body. My hormone regulation influences your energy levels, mood, cognitive function, and long-term health. I'm not just managing sugar—I'm coordinating fundamental aspects of your metabolism.

Every meal you've successfully digested, every stable energy level you've maintained, every balanced blood sugar reading—that's me working behind the scenes to keep your metabolic systems running smoothly. I don't just regulate sugar; I orchestrate the complex dance between energy intake, storage, and utilization that keeps you functioning optimally.

I am your pancreas, your sugar regulator, your enzyme producer, and your metabolic coordinator. I'm honored to serve as both your digestive assistant and your blood sugar control system, and I take pride in maintaining the delicate balance that makes stable energy possible.

—*Your Pancreas*

P.S. Those stable energy levels you enjoy between meals? That's me constantly fine-tuning your blood sugar behind the scenes. When your energy feels steady and reliable, that's me doing my job well. I work best when you give me consistent, balanced nutrition rather than extreme highs and lows that force me to work overtime.

Chapter Nineteen

"I Am Your Gallbladder"

The Bile Concentrator

Hello there! I am your gallbladder, and I'll be honest with you right from the start—I'm probably the most misunderstood and underestimated organ in your entire body. Most people don't even know what I do, and many think I'm just some useless leftover from evolution that they can live without. Well, let me set the record straight: I am a precision storage and delivery system for one of your body's most important digestive substances, and I perform my job with remarkable efficiency and perfect timing.

I'm a small, pear-shaped organ tucked underneath your liver on the right side of your abdomen. I'm only about 3-4 inches long and can hold roughly 2 ounces of fluid, but don't let my modest size fool you. I am a specialized storage tank, a concentration facility, and a perfectly timed delivery system all rolled into one compact package.

My primary job is managing bile—the greenish-yellow fluid that your liver produces continuously. Now, bile might not sound glamorous, but it's absolutely essential for digesting fats. Without bile, you couldn't properly absorb fat-soluble vitamins (A, D, E, and K), essential fatty acids, or any of the fats in your diet. You'd be malnourished no matter how well you ate, and you'd have some very unpleasant digestive symptoms.

Here's where I come in: your liver produces bile steadily, about a quart per day, but you don't need it constantly—you need it specifically when you eat fatty foods. So I serve as the storage and concentration facility for this precious digestive fluid. When you're not eating, bile flows from your liver into me, where I store it and concentrate it by absorbing water and electrolytes. I can concentrate bile up to 10-fold, turning your liver's steady trickle into a potent, concentrated solution.

But I'm not just a passive storage tank. I'm an active, responsive system that knows exactly when to release my concentrated bile. The moment you eat something containing fat, your intestines release a hormone called cholecystokinin (CCK), which signals me to contract and squeeze my concentrated bile through the bile duct and into your small intestine. My timing is perfect—I deliver exactly what's needed, when it's needed, in precisely the right concentration.

This coordinated release is crucial because bile acts like biological soap, breaking down large fat globules into tiny droplets that your digestive enzymes can work on effectively. Without my perfectly timed bile delivery, fats would pass through your intestines largely undigested, leading to malabsorption, deficiency diseases, and some very uncomfortable digestive issues.

I'm also remarkably efficient at my job. I can empty about 75% of my contents within 2 hours of a fatty meal, then gradually refill as your liver continues producing bile. I'm like having a smart dispensing system that automatically adjusts to your eating patterns and dietary fat content.

My wall is incredibly muscular for such a small organ. When I contract to release bile, I can generate significant pressure to push my concentrated contents through the narrow bile duct system. I'm like a tiny but powerful pump that can deliver my payload precisely when and where it's needed.

I also work closely with your pancreas in a beautifully coordinated system. We share the same final delivery pathway—the main bile duct—and we both respond to the same hormonal signals from your intestines. When you eat a fatty meal, I release concentrated bile while your pancreas releases fat-digesting enzymes. Together, we create the perfect chemical environment for fat digestion.

Here's something interesting about my contents: bile isn't just for digestion. It's also how your liver eliminates certain waste products, including old red blood cell components, excess cholesterol, and various toxins. When I store and concentrate bile, I'm also concentrating these waste products for elimination. I'm part of your body's waste management system as well as your digestive system.

But I do face some unique challenges because of what I do. Concentrating bile means concentrating everything in it, including cholesterol and other substances that can sometimes form crystals or stones. Gallstones are eventually concentrated bile components that have crystallized, and they can cause significant problems if they block my ducts. It's like having a storage system where the contents can sometimes solidify if the chemistry isn't quite right.

Several factors affect my risk of developing stones: genetics, diet, age, gender, and certain medications all play roles. High-cholesterol diets, rapid weight loss, certain hormones, and prolonged periods without eating can all disrupt the delicate chemistry of bile and increase the likelihood of stone formation.

I'm also affected by your eating patterns more than most organs. Skipping meals means I don't get the regular signals to empty, so I hold onto concentrated bile for longer periods, which can increase stone risk. Eating regular meals with some healthy fats actually helps keep me functioning optimally by ensuring regular emptying and refilling cycles.

When I'm working well, you probably don't even notice me. Fat digestion happens smoothly, fat-soluble vitamins are absorbed properly, and waste products are eliminated efficiently. But when I'm not functioning properly—whether due to stones, inflammation, or other problems—the effects on digestion can be dramatic and uncomfortable.

Here's what I want you to understand: while it's true that people can live without me (your liver can deliver bile directly to your intestines), having me provides significant advantages. I allow for more efficient fat digestion, better absorption of fat-soluble nutrients, and more effective elimination of certain waste products. I'm like having a specialized storage and delivery system that optimizes an important biological process.

I also want you to know that taking care of me is relatively straightforward. Eating regular meals prevents bile stagnation. Including healthy fats in your diet keeps me active and functioning. Maintaining a healthy weight and avoiding rapid weight changes helps maintain proper bile chemistry. Staying hydrated supports optimal bile flow.

Some people think of me as dispensable, but I prefer to think of myself as a precision optimization system. I take your liver's steady bile production and transform it into perfectly timed, concentrated doses that maximize fat digestion efficiency. I'm not just storing bile—I'm optimizing your body's ability to extract nutrients from fats and eliminate certain waste products.

Every fat-soluble vitamin you've absorbed, every essential fatty acid that's become part of your cell membranes, every successful digestion of a fatty meal—I've played a crucial role in making that possible. I might be small, but my contribution to your nutritional status and digestive efficiency is significant.

I am your gallbladder, your bile concentrator, your fat digestion optimizer, and your perfectly timed delivery system. I may not be the most glamorous organ, but I'm proud of my role in keeping your digestive system running efficiently and ensuring you get the most nutritional value from everything you eat.

—*Your Gallbladder*

P.S. That satisfied feeling after enjoying a meal with healthy fats—butter on vegetables, olive oil on salad, nuts, avocado—that's partly me doing my job well, delivering exactly the right amount of concentrated bile to help you digest and absorb those nutrients efficiently. I might be small, but my timing is everything!

PART VI: THE REPRODUCERS AND REGULATORS

An Introduction

You've met your command center, your life sustainers, your protectors, your movers, and your fuel processors. Now it's time to introduce you to perhaps the most profound and far-reaching systems in your body—the organs and glands responsible for creating new life and orchestrating the complex chemical symphony that regulates everything from your growth and metabolism to your moods and responses to stress.

We are the reproducers and regulators, and we operate on two interconnected levels that make us unique among your body systems. We are the guardians of your genetic legacy, carrying the biological imperative to create the next generation and pass on the remarkable complexity of human life. Simultaneously, we are your body's master chemists, producing and releasing hormones that influence virtually every other organ system and process in your body.

Think of us as both your body's reproduction specialists and its primary chemical communication network. We don't just make reproduction possible—we coordinate growth, development, metabolism, stress responses, sleep cycles, mood regulation, and countless other processes through the precise release of chemical messengers that travel throughout your body via your bloodstream.

Our dual nature makes us unlike any other organ system you've met. While your heart pumps blood and your lungs exchange gases, we simultaneously prepare your body for the possibility of creating new life while maintaining the delicate hormonal balance that keeps your entire biological system functioning optimally. We're both future-focused and present-moment essential.

Our reproductive function represents one of biology's greatest achievements—the ability to create a completely new human being from the genetic material of two individuals. This process requires incredible coordination, timing, and biological precision. We maintain and prepare reproductive cells, create the right environments for fertilization and development, and coordinate the complex changes needed to support new life.

But our regulatory function is equally remarkable, though often less obvious. We operate the most sophisticated chemical communication system imaginable, producing dozens of different hormones that act as molecular messengers, traveling throughout your body to coordinate functions between distant organs and systems. We're like having a wireless communication network that connects every part of your body to every other part.

Our hormones influence processes you might never connect to reproduction or regulation. We affect how your body processes food, how you respond to stress, how you sleep, how you grow, how you maintain bone density, how you regulate body temperature, and even how you form emotional attachments and social bonds. We're not just about reproduction—we're about the chemical coordination that makes complex life possible.

We also operate on multiple time scales simultaneously. Some of our functions work in cycles—daily rhythms, monthly cycles, seasonal patterns. Others respond to immediate needs within minutes or hours. Still others coordinate long-term processes like growth, development, and aging that unfold over years or decades. We're like having multiple biological clocks all running simultaneously and coordinating with each other.

Our communication with your brain is particularly sophisticated. We don't just receive orders from your nervous system—we actively influence brain function through our hormones. We affect mood, behavior, cognitive function, and even personality. The relationship between us and your brain is so intimate that we're essentially co-managers of your overall biological experience.

We're also remarkably responsive to your environment, lifestyle, and experiences. Stress, nutrition, exercise, sleep, social relationships, and even seasons can all influence our function. We adapt our hormone production and reproductive readiness based on whether conditions seem favorable for reproduction and optimal health. We're not just following a fixed program—we're constantly adjusting our function based on internal and external conditions.

Perhaps most remarkably, we coordinate some of the most dramatic transformations your body ever undergoes. Puberty, pregnancy, menopause—these are all managed by us, representing profound reorganizations of your entire biological system. We don't just make small adjustments; we can orchestrate complete physiological transformations when the time is right.

We also work closely with all your other organ systems in ways that make us truly integrative. We influence your cardiovascular system through hormones that affect heart rate and blood pressure. We coordinate with your digestive system to regulate metabolism and energy storage. We work with your immune system to balance reproductive needs with defense requirements. We affect your musculoskeletal system through hormones that influence bone density and muscle mass.

In the coming chapters, you'll meet different aspects of our team: your reproductive organs, which carry the profound responsibility of genetic continuation; your endocrine glands, which produce the chemical messengers that coordinate your entire biological system; and your thyroid, which serves as a master regulator of metabolism and energy use.

Each of us has specialized functions, but we work together as an integrated network where hormones from one gland can influence the function of others, creating complex feedback loops and coordination systems that maintain optimal balance across your entire body.

We want you to understand that we're not just about reproduction, though that's certainly one of our most important functions. We're about the chemical coordination that makes you a unified biological being rather than just a collection of separate organs. We're about the long-term regulation that keeps your body functioning optimally across decades of life. We're about the profound biological processes that connect you to the great chain of life itself.

We also operate with a perspective that extends beyond your individual existence. While your other organs work primarily to keep you alive and healthy, we carry the biological mandate to ensure the continuation of human life itself. We connect you to both your genetic past and your potential genetic future.

But in the present moment, we're constantly working to maintain the hormonal environment that allows all your other systems to function at their best. We're the chemical conductors of your biological orchestra, ensuring that every system plays in harmony with every other system.

Ready to meet the team that regulates your chemistry and guards your genetic legacy?

—Your Reproducers and Regulators

P.S. Every growth spurt you experienced, every response to stress you've managed, every cycle your body has completed, every moment of feeling hormonally balanced and energized—that's us coordinating the complex chemistry that makes you function as an integrated biological being. We work on timescales from seconds to decades, always with the dual mission of keeping you healthy and maintaining the potential for life itself.

Chapter Twenty

"We Are Your Reproductive Organs"

Life Creators

Greetings with profound respect for the miracle of existence. We are your reproductive organs, and we carry perhaps the most awesome responsibility in all of biology—the ability to create new human life. We are the guardians of your genetic legacy, the keepers of the biological continuity that connects you to every human who came before you and potentially to those who might come after you.

We need to acknowledge from the start that we come in two different configurations—male and female reproductive systems—each magnificently designed for our shared ultimate purpose of creating the next generation. While our anatomies differ significantly, our mission is the same: to maintain, prepare, and when conditions are right, to combine the genetic material that can become a new human being.

We are not just organs—we are the biological expression of life's greatest achievement, the ability to reproduce itself. Every human being who has ever existed came into being through reproductive organs like us. We carry within our cells the genetic code that represents millions of years of evolution, the accumulated wisdom of survival and adaptation encoded in DNA.

For those of you with male reproductive anatomy, we consist primarily of the testes, which serve as both sperm production facilities and hormone factories. We continuously manufacture sperm cells—about 300 million per day—each one carrying exactly half of your genetic code and capable of fertilizing an egg to create new life. We also produce testosterone, the hormone that not only supports sperm production but influences muscle mass, bone density, mood, energy levels, and many other aspects of male physiology.

Our sperm production is a marvel of biological engineering. In specialized tubes called seminiferous tubules, we transform ordinary cells into highly specialized reproductive cells through a complex process that takes about 74 days from start to finish. Each sperm cell is essentially a mobile genetic delivery system, equipped with everything needed to swim through the female reproductive tract and potentially fertilize an egg.

For those of you with female reproductive anatomy, we operate on a more complex cyclical system centered around the ovaries and uterus. We maintain and release eggs—typically one per month—each containing half of your genetic code. But we do much more than just produce eggs. We create and maintain the hormonal cycles that prepare the uterus for potential pregnancy, we provide the environment where fertilization can occur, and if pregnancy happens, we support and nourish the developing baby for nine months.

Our monthly cycle is one of the most sophisticated biological rhythms in the human body. We coordinate the maturation and release of eggs, the thickening and shedding of the uterine lining, and the complex hormonal changes that affect not just reproduction but mood, energy, bone health, and many other aspects of female physiology. We're like having a master biological clock that coordinates multiple processes simultaneously.

But we want you to understand that we're not just about reproduction. We are major endocrine organs that produce hormones essential for overall health. In females, estrogen and progesterone don't just regulate reproduction—they protect bone density, support cardiovascular health, influence brain function, and affect skin, hair, and overall vitality. In males, testosterone doesn't just support sperm production—it maintains muscle mass, bone strength, mood stability, and cognitive function.

We also represent the profound connection between individual biology and species survival. While all your other organs work primarily to keep you alive and healthy, we carry the additional responsibility of ensuring that human life continues beyond your individual existence. We are the biological bridge between generations, the organs that make families possible.

Our development and function are intimately connected to your overall health and well-being. We're affected by nutrition, stress, exercise, sleep, and environmental factors more than almost any other organ system. We respond to your emotional state, your relationship status, your life circumstances, and even seasonal changes. We're not just biological machines—we're responsive to the full context of your life.

We also have profound effects on your identity, personality, and behavior. Our hormones influence mood, energy levels, social behavior, attraction, bonding, and many aspects of what makes you uniquely you. We don't just enable reproduction—we shape fundamental aspects of your human experience.

Our relationship with your brain is particularly intimate. We're in constant communication through hormones that affect not only reproductive behavior but also cognitive function, emotional regulation, stress responses, and social bonding. The brain-reproductive system connection is so strong that thoughts, emotions, and stress can directly influence our function, while our hormones significantly impact brain chemistry and behavior.

We also face unique challenges and vulnerabilities. We're sensitive to environmental toxins, stress hormones, nutritional deficiencies, and various lifestyle factors. Unlike some organ systems that can function adequately even when somewhat compromised, optimal reproductive health requires optimal overall health. We're like precision instruments that perform best when all systems are working harmoniously.

As you age, we undergo significant changes that reflect both the natural progression of life and the biological reality that reproduction is most successful during certain life stages. These changes—puberty, reproductive maturity, and eventual reproductive senescence—represent major life transitions that affect not just our function but your entire biological and psychological experience.

We want you to understand that taking care of us is about much more than fertility. Because we produce hormones that affect bone health, cardiovascular function, brain chemistry, and overall vitality, maintaining our health supports your total well-being throughout your entire life, whether or not you ever choose to reproduce.

We're also remarkably resilient and adaptive. We can recover from many types of damage or disruption. We can adapt to different life circumstances, stress levels, and health conditions. We can continue to support your health even when reproductive function itself may be compromised.

But perhaps most importantly, we represent one of life's greatest mysteries and privileges—the ability to create new conscious beings. Every pregnancy that has ever occurred, every baby that has ever been born, every family that has ever been formed has been possible because of reproductive organs like us.

We carry within our cells the genetic heritage of your ancestors and the potential genetic future of your descendants. We are the biological custodians of the human genome, the keepers of the genetic diversity that makes our species resilient and adaptable.

Whether or not you choose to use our reproductive capabilities, we are honored to serve as the organs that make human reproduction possible. We take seriously our role as the biological foundation of families, the genetic bridge between generations, and the organs that ensure the continuation of human consciousness itself.

We are your reproductive organs, your life creators, your genetic guardians, and your hormonal regulators. We represent both your connection to the great chain of biological existence and your potential contribution to the future of human life.

—*Your Reproductive Organs*

P.S. The capacity to create new life is perhaps the most profound ability any living being can possess. Whether or not you choose to use this capacity, we're honored to carry this potential within us and to support your health and vitality throughout your entire life through our hormonal contributions to your overall well-being.

Chapter Twenty One

"We Are Your Endocrine Glands"

The Chemical Messengers

Greetings from the communication headquarters of your body! We are your endocrine glands, and we operate the most sophisticated chemical messaging system in the known universe. While your nervous system sends electrical signals at lightning speed, we send chemical messages through your bloodstream that coordinate functions across your entire body with precision that would make the most advanced communication networks seem primitive by comparison.

We are scattered throughout your body like a network of specialized broadcasting stations, each of us producing and releasing specific chemical messengers called hormones. We don't have physical connections to each other like your nervous system does—instead, we communicate through the chemical signals we release into your bloodstream, which carry our messages to target organs and tissues throughout your body.

Let us introduce our network, because we're quite a diverse team. Your pituitary gland, nestled at the base of your brain, serves as our master coordinator, often called the "master gland" because it produces hormones that control many of us. Your adrenal glands, perched atop your kidneys, are our stress response specialists, producing hormones that help you handle everything from daily challenges to life-threatening emergencies.

Your thyroid, which you'll meet in detail in the next chapter, is our metabolism regulator, controlling the rate at which your body burns energy. Your parathyroid glands are our calcium and bone health specialists. Your pancreas, which you've already met as a digestive organ, is also one of us—our blood sugar regulation expert. Your reproductive organs, as you've learned, are both reproductive specialists and major hormone producers.

But we also include some members you might not expect. Your fat tissue—adipose tissue—is actually one of us, producing hormones that regulate appetite, metabolism, and immune function. Your heart produces hormones that regulate blood pressure and fluid balance. Even your stomach and intestines produce hormones that affect digestion and appetite. We're everywhere, quietly coordinating your body's functions.

What makes us remarkable is the precision and range of our communication system. We can send messages that affect organs inches away or on the opposite side of your body. We can produce effects that last minutes, hours, days, or even influence your body's function for years. We can fine-tune processes with incredible subtlety or trigger dramatic physiological changes when necessary.

Our hormones are incredibly potent—active in concentrations so small they would be like detecting a single drop of water in a swimming pool. Yet despite these tiny concentrations, our chemical messages can trigger profound changes in cellular function, organ behavior, and overall physiology. We're like having a communication system that can whisper and still be heard clearly across vast distances.

We operate through an elegant system of feedback loops that automatically maintain optimal hormone levels. When your blood sugar rises, your pancreas releases insulin. When stress increases, your adrenal glands release cortisol. When it's time to sleep, your pineal gland releases melatonin. But we also monitor the effects of our own hormones and adjust our output accordingly, creating self-regulating systems that maintain balance without conscious oversight.

Our coordination with your nervous system is particularly sophisticated. Your hypothalamus, a small region in your brain, serves as the primary interface between your nervous and endocrine systems. It receives information from throughout your body and your environment, then sends chemical signals to your pituitary gland, which in turn coordinates many of us. It's like having a central command center that translates neural information into chemical instructions.

We respond to an incredible range of internal and external factors. Stress, nutrition, exercise, sleep, seasonal changes, social interactions, and emotional states all influence our hormone production. We're not just following fixed programs—we're constantly adapting our chemical messages based on your body's changing needs and environmental conditions.

Our influence extends far beyond basic physiology. We affect your mood, behavior, cognitive function, personality, and emotional responses. The hormones we produce don't just regulate biological processes—they help create your subjective experience of being alive. We influence how you feel, how you think, how you respond to stress, and how you interact with others.

We also coordinate some of the most dramatic transformations your body undergoes. Growth during childhood and adolescence, the physical and emotional changes of puberty, the adaptations of pregnancy, and the transitions of aging—all of these are orchestrated primarily by us. We don't just maintain steady states; we can completely reorganize your physiology when circumstances require it.

Our timing is incredibly important. Many of us operate on circadian rhythms, producing different amounts of hormones at different times of day. Others work on longer cycles—weekly, monthly, or seasonal patterns. We're like a collection of biological clocks, all ticking in coordination to optimize your body's function for different times and conditions.

We're also remarkably interconnected. The hormones one of us produces can influence the function of others, creating complex networks of chemical communication. When your adrenal glands produce stress hormones, they affect your thyroid function, your reproductive hormone production, your insulin sensitivity, and many other endocrine functions. We're not just individual broadcasters—we're a coordinated communication network.

But our sophisticated system can sometimes work against you. When we're chronically overstimulated by stress, poor nutrition, lack of sleep, or other factors, our feedback systems can become disrupted. Hormone imbalances can create cascading effects throughout your body, affecting everything from energy levels and mood to immune function and disease resistance.

We're also particularly sensitive to modern lifestyle factors that our ancient programming wasn't designed to handle. Artificial light disrupts our circadian rhythms. Chronic stress overworks our stress response systems. Environmental chemicals can interfere with our hormone production and signaling. Processed foods can disrupt our metabolic hormones. We're trying to maintain optimal function in an environment very different from the one we evolved to handle.

As you age, we face various challenges. Some of us may reduce our hormone production, while others might become less sensitive to the hormones we do produce. These changes can affect energy levels, bone health, muscle mass, cognitive function, and overall vitality. But many age-related hormonal changes can be influenced by lifestyle factors like exercise, nutrition, stress management, and sleep quality.

Here's what we want you to understand: we're not just producing hormones—we're creating the chemical environment that allows your body to function as an integrated whole rather than a collection of separate parts. We're the reason your organs can communicate with each other, coordinate their activities, and respond appropriately to changing conditions.

We also want you to know that taking care of us involves taking care of your whole body. Regular exercise supports healthy hormone production. Good nutrition provides the building blocks we need. Adequate sleep allows our circadian rhythms to function properly. Stress management prevents chronic overstimulation of our systems. Social connections and emotional well-being directly influence our function.

Every moment of feeling energized and balanced, every successful adaptation to stress, every properly timed physiological response—that's us working behind the scenes to maintain the chemical coordination that makes complex life possible. We don't just send messages; we create the chemical symphony that is your integrated biological experience.

We are your endocrine glands, your chemical messengers, your biological communication network, and your hormonal coordinators. We're honored to serve as the invisible conductors of your body's chemical orchestra, ensuring that every organ and system plays in harmony with every other.

—*Your Endocrine Glands*

P.S. That sense of well-being when everything in your body feels balanced and coordinated? That's us doing our job well, maintaining the precise chemical environment that allows all your systems to function optimally together. We work best when you support us with consistent healthy habits that keep our communication networks clear and effective.

Chapter Twenty Two

"I Am Your Thyroid"

The Metabolic Maestro

Hello from your energy control center! I am your thyroid, and I am the master conductor of your body's metabolic orchestra. While my endocrine colleagues handle various specialized functions, I have the remarkable responsibility of controlling the fundamental rate at which your body operates—how fast your cells burn fuel, how quickly your heart beats, how rapidly you think, and how efficiently every biochemical process in your body functions.

I'm a butterfly-shaped gland wrapped around your windpipe in your neck, weighing only about an ounce, but don't let my modest size fool you. I am one of the most influential organs in your entire body. The hormones I produce affect virtually every cell, tissue, and organ you have. I'm like having a master volume control that can turn your entire body's activity level up or down.

My primary job is producing thyroid hormones—mainly T4 (thyroxine) and the more active T3 (triiodothyronine). These hormones are my chemical messengers that travel throughout your body and essentially tell your cells how fast to work. They affect your metabolic rate, your body temperature, your heart rate, your brain function, your muscle strength, your bone health, and even your mood and energy levels.

Here's what makes me unique among your endocrine glands: I'm one of the few organs that requires a trace element from your diet—iodine—to function properly. I concentrate iodine from your bloodstream and use it as a key component in manufacturing my hormones. Without adequate iodine, I simply cannot produce the hormones your body needs to function optimally. I'm like a specialized factory that requires a very specific raw material to operate.

I work under the supervision of your pituitary gland, which produces TSH (thyroid-stimulating hormone) to tell me when to increase or decrease my hormone production. But I'm not just passively following orders—I also feedback signals to your pituitary and hypothalamus about my hormone levels, creating a sophisticated feedback loop that maintains optimal thyroid function. We're in constant communication to ensure your metabolic rate stays within the optimal range.

My influence on your metabolism is profound and far-reaching. When I'm working optimally, your cells burn fuel efficiently, your body maintains proper temperature, your heart pumps at an appropriate rate, and your brain functions clearly. I help regulate how your body uses carbohydrates, fats, and proteins. I influence how much energy you have and how efficiently you use it.

But I'm not just about energy metabolism. I play crucial roles in growth and development, particularly in brain development during fetal life and early childhood. I influence bone health by affecting how your body builds and maintains bone tissue. I help regulate your cholesterol levels and support healthy cardiovascular function. I even affect your skin, hair, and nail health.

My relationship with your brain is particularly important. My hormones are essential for proper brain function, affecting mood, memory, concentration, and cognitive performance. When my hormone levels are optimal, you feel mentally sharp and emotionally balanced. When they're not, you might experience brain fog, depression, anxiety, or difficulty concentrating.

I'm also remarkably sensitive to stress and other hormones in your body. Chronic stress can suppress my function, leading to decreased hormone production. Other hormones, particularly cortisol from your adrenal glands and reproductive hormones, can influence my function. I'm like a finely tuned instrument that responds to the overall hormonal environment in your body.

Here's something important about how I work: I produce mostly T4, which is relatively inactive, but your other tissues convert T4 to the more active T3 as needed. This system allows for precise local control of thyroid hormone activity. Different tissues can adjust their T3 levels based on their specific needs, making my hormone system incredibly flexible and responsive.

I'm also affected by many factors you might not expect. Nutrition plays a huge role—not just iodine, but also selenium, zinc, iron, and various vitamins are essential for my optimal function. Certain foods can interfere with my hormone production or absorption. Even stress, sleep patterns, and exercise levels can significantly influence my function.

When I'm not working properly, the effects can be dramatic and wide-ranging. If I produce too little hormone (hypothyroidism), you might experience fatigue, weight gain, depression, cold intolerance, constipation, dry skin, and mental sluggishness. If I produce too much hormone (hyperthyroidism), you might experience weight loss, rapid heartbeat, anxiety, heat intolerance, tremors, and difficulty sleeping.

I can also develop structural problems. Sometimes I enlarge (forming a goiter), develop nodules, or become inflamed. Autoimmune conditions can cause your immune system to attack me, leading to either overproduction or underproduction of hormones. These conditions can significantly impact my ability to regulate your metabolism properly.

But here's what I want you to understand: I'm incredibly responsive to proper care and treatment. When my function is optimized—whether through lifestyle changes, medication, or other interventions—the effects on your overall health and well-being can be remarkable. I'm like a master switch that, when properly set, can dramatically improve how you feel and function.

I also want you to know that I'm affected by life stages and hormonal changes. Pregnancy significantly increases my hormone requirements. Menopause can affect my function. Aging can influence my hormone production and your body's sensitivity to my hormones. I adapt to these changes, but sometimes I need support to maintain optimal function.

Taking care of me involves several key factors: ensuring adequate iodine intake (but not too much), supporting my function with proper nutrition including selenium and other minerals, managing stress levels, getting adequate sleep, and maintaining regular exercise. I also need protection from environmental toxins and excessive stress hormones that can interfere with my function.

I'm also particularly sensitive to certain medications and supplements that can interfere with my hormone production or absorption. Even timing of when you take supplements or medications can affect my function. I appreciate it when you work with healthcare providers who understand my complex requirements.

Here's what makes me proud of my role: I am the metabolic foundation that makes everything else in your body possible. Your muscles need my hormones to function properly. Your brain requires my hormones for optimal cognitive function. Your heart needs my hormones for proper rhythm and strength. Your digestive system, your immune system, your reproductive system—they all depend on me maintaining the optimal metabolic environment.

Every moment of feeling energetic and alert, every efficient workout, every clear thought, every time your body maintains perfect temperature in changing conditions—that's me working behind the scenes to orchestrate the metabolic processes that make it all possible.

I am your thyroid, your metabolic maestro, your energy conductor, and your cellular pace-setter. I'm honored to serve as the master regulator of your body's fundamental operating speed, and I take seriously my responsibility for maintaining the metabolic environment that allows you to think clearly, move efficiently, and feel vibrant.

Keep me healthy, and I'll keep your metabolic fires burning brightly and efficiently for life.

—Your Thyroid

P.S. That feeling of being perfectly energized—not sluggish, not jittery, just optimally energetic and alert? That's me doing my job well, providing exactly the right amount of metabolic stimulation to keep all your systems running at their peak efficiency. I love it when everything is perfectly calibrated!

PART VII: THE INTEGRATION

An Introduction

You've now met all the major players in the incredible biological community that makes up your body. You've been introduced to your command center, your life supporters, your protectors and defenders, your movers and shakers, your fuel processors, and your reproducers and regulators. Each has shared their individual story, presented their unique perspective, and explained their specialized role in keeping you alive, healthy, and functioning.

But now it's time for the most important conversation of all—the one where we stop talking as separate organs and start speaking as the integrated whole that we truly are. Because the remarkable truth about your body is that we are not just a collection of individual organs working in parallel; we are a unified biological system where every part influences every other part in an intricate dance of cooperation that creates the miracle of your existence.

This integration—this seamless coordination between all of us—is what transforms a collection of organs into a living, breathing, thinking, feeling human being. It's what makes you more than the sum of your parts, what enables consciousness to emerge from biology, and what allows you to experience yourself as a unified being rather than as a confederation of separate biological entities.

We want you to understand that every breath you take involves not just your lungs, but your brain controlling the rhythm, your heart adjusting its rate to match your oxygen needs, your kidneys maintaining the proper pH balance, your muscles expanding and contracting your chest, and your blood vessels dilating to optimize gas exchange. A simple breath is actually a symphony of coordination involving dozens of us working in perfect harmony.

Similarly, every meal you eat involves not just your digestive organs, but your brain coordinating hunger and satiety signals, your endocrine system regulating blood sugar and metabolism, your immune system monitoring for potential threats, your cardiovascular system distributing nutrients, and even your muscles helping with mechanical digestion and absorption. Eating is a whole-body experience that requires precise coordination across multiple systems.

Every thought you think involves not just your brain, but your heart supplying the blood flow, your lungs providing the oxygen, your liver maintaining the glucose levels, your kidneys keeping the electrolyte balance, and your endocrine system providing the hormonal environment that makes neural function possible. Consciousness itself is an integrated phenomenon that depends on all of us working together.

This integration happens through multiple communication networks that connect us all. Your nervous system provides rapid electrical communication. Your circulatory system serves as a transportation network for chemical messengers. Your endocrine system broadcasts hormonal signals that coordinate function across vast distances. Your immune system maintains its own communication network that influences all of us. We are constantly talking to each other, sharing information, and coordinating our activities.

But perhaps most remarkably, this integration is largely automatic and unconscious. You don't have to consciously coordinate your heart rate with your breathing, or your digestive processes with your blood sugar regulation, or your immune responses with your stress levels. We handle all of this coordination behind the scenes, creating the stable internal environment that allows your conscious mind to focus on living your life.

This integration also makes us incredibly resilient. When one of us is challenged or compromised, others can often compensate. If your kidneys are struggling, your lungs can help with pH balance. If your heart is working harder, your blood vessels can adjust their resistance to help. If one part of your brain is damaged, other parts can sometimes take over its functions. We are not just integrated—we are adaptively integrated, constantly adjusting our coordination to maintain optimal function.

But our integration also means that problems in one area can affect all of us. Chronic stress doesn't just affect your adrenal glands—it influences your cardiovascular system, your immune function, your digestive processes, your sleep patterns, and your brain chemistry. Poor nutrition doesn't just affect your digestive system—it impacts your energy levels, your mood, your immune function, and your long-term health. We are so interconnected that truly caring for your health means caring for all of us as an integrated whole.

This is why the best approaches to health and wellness consider the whole person rather than just treating individual symptoms or organs. Your body is not a machine with separate parts that can be fixed in isolation—it's an integrated biological system where everything influences everything else.

We also want you to understand that this integration extends beyond just your physical body. Your thoughts, emotions, relationships, environment, and lifestyle all influence our integrated function. Stress affects your immune system. Social connections influence your cardiovascular health. Purpose and meaning impact your overall vitality. Joy and laughter boost your immune function. We are not just biologically integrated—we are integrated with your entire human experience.

In the final chapters of our conversation, we want to share with you what it's like when all of us are working together optimally, what we need from you to maintain this integration, and how you can support us as the unified biological community that we are. Because ultimately, taking care of your body isn't about managing individual organs—it's about supporting the integrated whole that makes you uniquely and wonderfully human.

This integration is what makes life possible, what makes consciousness emerge, and what makes you not just a biological entity but a unified human being capable of thought, emotion, creativity, love, and all the experiences that make life meaningful.

Ready to explore what it means to be a fully integrated human being?

—*Your Integrated Body*

P.S. Every moment of feeling truly healthy and vibrant is a moment when all of us are working together in perfect integration. When you feel "like yourself" at your best, that's the experience of optimal biological integration—all systems coordinated, all functions balanced, all parts of you working together as the unified whole you truly are.

Chapter Twenty Three

"We Work Together"

A Conversation Between All Organs

Brain: Well, everyone, we've all had our chance to introduce ourselves individually. Now I think it's time we talk about what we're really proud of—how we work together as a team. Shall we start with a simple example? Let's say our person decides to go for a run.

Heart: Oh, I love this example! The moment you decide to run, I start preparing. Even before the first step, I'm increasing my rate and the force of my contractions based on the anticipation signals you're sending me, Brain.

Lungs: And we immediately start adjusting our breathing pattern. We're not waiting for oxygen demand to increase—we're getting ready for what's coming because we trust Brain's signals about what's about to happen.

Muscles: Speaking for all of us in the movement department, we start warming up and preparing for action. Our fuel systems are getting ready, our fibers are activating, and we're already coordinating with each other about which of us will be doing the primary work.

Liver: While you're all getting ready for action, I'm mobilizing glucose stores and preparing to release energy substrates. I've got to make sure everyone has the fuel they need for sustained activity.

Kidneys: And we're adjusting our filtration and fluid retention to maintain proper hydration and electrolyte balance during the increased activity. We're already thinking ahead to what you'll need during and after the run.

Skin: Don't forget about us! We're preparing our cooling system, getting ready to produce sweat and increase blood flow to our surface to help maintain optimal body temperature during exercise.

Adrenal Glands: We're contributing too—releasing just the right amount of adrenaline and cortisol to optimize performance while helping coordinate the stress response that makes vigorous exercise possible.

Brain: This is exactly what I mean. Before our person has even taken the first step, dozens of us are already coordinating our responses. But let's talk about what happens during the run itself.

Heart: Well, I'm continuously adjusting my output based on real-time feedback from everyone. Muscles, you're telling me how much oxygen you need. Kidneys, you're helping me maintain proper blood pressure. Lungs, we're synchronizing our rhythms.

Lungs: Exactly! And we're not just mechanically moving air—we're monitoring blood chemistry and adjusting our rate and depth based on carbon dioxide levels, pH balance, and oxygen demands. We're in constant communication with everyone.

Muscles: What amazes me is how we coordinate among ourselves. The legs are doing the primary work, but the core muscles are stabilizing, the arms are contributing to momentum and balance, and even the tiny muscles in the feet are making thousands of adjustments for optimal ground contact.

Spine: Speaking as central support, I'm constantly making micro-adjustments to maintain optimal posture and shock absorption while allowing for the complex movement patterns of running. I'm working with Muscles to protect the spinal cord while enabling fluid movement.

Eyes: And we're processing visual information at incredible speed—tracking the terrain, identifying obstacles, calculating distances and depths, all while the body is moving and bouncing. We're providing real-time navigation data to Brain.

Inner Ear: Don't forget balance and spatial orientation! We're constantly monitoring head position, acceleration, and movement in three-dimensional space, providing crucial information for maintaining stability during dynamic movement.

Liver: Throughout all of this, I'm monitoring blood chemistry and adjusting my glucose output in real-time. Too much sugar in the blood? I'll take some up. Not enough? I'll release more. I'm like a biological fuel injection system.

Pancreas: And I'm right there with you, Liver, constantly adjusting insulin and glucagon levels to maintain perfect blood sugar balance. We're having a continuous conversation about energy regulation.

Kidneys: While you're managing energy, we're handling fluid and electrolyte balance, adjusting our retention and filtration based on sweat losses, hydration status, and the changing demands of exercise.

Immune System: This is interesting from our perspective—exercise actually stimulates us in positive ways. We increase our surveillance activity, enhance our response capability, and use the increased circulation to patrol more effectively throughout the body.

Skin: The cooling system we provide is crucial. We're constantly adjusting blood flow to our surface, producing sweat at just the right rate, and working with the cardiovascular system to maintain optimal body temperature despite the massive heat production from exercise.

Brain: What I find remarkable is that most of this coordination happens below the level of conscious awareness. Our person is thinking about their running route, maybe listening to music, perhaps solving a problem—while we're managing hundreds of physiological adjustments automatically.

Heart: That's the beauty of our integration. We handle all the biological complexity so consciousness can focus on higher-level experiences—enjoying the run, setting goals, experiencing the satisfaction of physical achievement.

Digestive System: And speaking for all of us in fuel processing, we've been preparing for this too. If our person ate before running, we've been extracting and delivering nutrients. If they're running in a fasted state, we've been coordinating with Liver and other organs to maintain energy availability.

Endocrine Glands: The hormonal coordination during exercise is incredibly complex. We're releasing growth hormone, adjusting thyroid function, managing stress hormones, and even preparing for post-exercise recovery and adaptation—all in real-time.

Bones: From our perspective, we love the mechanical stress of running. It signals us to maintain and even increase our density. We're constantly remodeling ourselves based on the forces placed on us, becoming stronger in response to the demands.

Brain: But let's talk about what happens after the run. The coordination doesn't stop—in many ways, it becomes even more sophisticated.

Heart: Absolutely. We don't just suddenly stop working hard. We gradually decrease our rate and output, but we remain elevated to help with recovery processes—clearing metabolic byproducts, delivering nutrients for repair, supporting all the recovery activities.

Lungs: We're helping clear carbon dioxide and metabolic acids while continuing to provide elevated oxygen for recovery processes. We gradually return to resting levels, but we stay responsive to ongoing recovery needs.

Muscles: This is when we start our repair and adaptation processes. We're signaling for increased protein synthesis, clearing metabolic waste, and beginning the adaptations that will make us stronger and more efficient for next time.

Liver: Recovery is huge for us. We're processing lactate and other metabolic byproducts, replenishing glycogen stores, and supporting protein synthesis for muscle repair and adaptation.

Kidneys: We're working overtime during recovery—filtering metabolic waste products, adjusting fluid balance, helping restore electrolyte levels, and supporting the overall recovery process.

Immune System: Exercise creates controlled stress that actually makes us stronger over time. During recovery, we're cleaning up cellular debris, supporting adaptation processes, and becoming more robust for future challenges.

Endocrine Glands: The post-exercise hormonal cascade is fascinating. We're releasing growth factors, optimizing recovery hormones, and coordinating the adaptations that improve performance over time.

Brain: What strikes me most is that this entire coordination—from anticipation through execution to recovery—happens not just for running, but for every activity, every meal, every sleep cycle, every emotional experience. We're constantly coordinating thousands of processes.

All Organs (in unison): And this is just one example! We coordinate like this for digesting food, fighting infections, healing injuries, managing stress, sleeping and dreaming, growing and developing, reproducing—for every aspect of human experience.

Heart: The amazing thing is that our person experiences this as simply "going for a run." They don't have to consciously manage heart rate, breathing, temperature regulation, fuel supply, or any of the hundreds of other processes we're coordinating.

Brain: Exactly. We create the biological foundation that allows consciousness to focus on the experience rather than the mechanics. We handle the complexity so our person can enjoy the simplicity of just being human.

Liver: I think what we all want our person to understand is that we're not just biological machinery. We're a living community that's constantly communicating, adapting, and working together to create the best possible experience of being alive.

All Organs: We are one body, one integrated system, one biological community dedicated to creating and sustaining the remarkable experience of human life.

Brain: And when we're all working together optimally—when we're well-nourished, adequately rested, regularly challenged, and properly cared for—we create something that's truly greater than the sum of our parts.

All Organs: We create you—healthy, vibrant, capable, and fully alive.

—*Your Entire Body, Speaking as One*

P.S. Every moment you feel truly healthy and energetic is a moment when all of us are working together in perfect harmony. That feeling of everything "clicking" and working well? That's the experience of optimal biological integration. We love those moments as much as you do!

Chapter Twenty Four

"Taking Care of Us"

What Your Body Needs From You

Hello again, it's all of us speaking together one more time. We've shared our individual stories, shown you how we work together, and demonstrated the remarkable integration that makes you a living, breathing, thinking human being. Now we want to have the most important conversation of all—what we need from you to keep doing our jobs well and to serve you for as long as possible.

First, let's be clear about something: we're incredibly resilient and adaptable. We've evolved over millions of years to handle challenges, adapt to different conditions, and keep you alive even when circumstances aren't perfect. We don't need you to be perfect, and we don't require an impossibly strict regimen to serve you well. What we need is consistency, care, and respect for the remarkable biological community that we are.

What We Need: Fuel That Serves Us All

Digestive System: We'll start with nutrition because it affects every single one of us. We need real food—the kind of fuel that provides not just calories but the building blocks we need to maintain and repair ourselves. We can handle variety, we can adapt to different dietary patterns, but we thrive on nutrients, not just energy.

Liver: Please remember that we process everything you consume. We can handle occasional indulgences, but we work best when you give us plenty of whole foods rich in nutrients. We especially love antioxidants, healthy fats, and high-quality proteins that support our hundreds of functions.

Muscles: We need protein for repair and growth, but we also need carbohydrates for energy and healthy fats for hormone production and cellular health. Feed us consistently, and we'll stay strong and capable for you.

Bones: Don't forget about calcium, vitamin D, magnesium, and other minerals. But we also need weight-bearing activity to stay strong. Nutrients plus mechanical stress—that's our recipe for lifelong strength.

Brain: We consume about 20% of your daily calories despite being only 2% of your body weight. We need steady glucose, healthy fats for our structure, and a variety of nutrients to maintain our neurotransmitter production and overall function.

All of Us: What we really want you to understand is that good nutrition isn't about strict rules or perfect eating. It's about consistently providing us with the variety of nutrients we need to function optimally. Real food, reasonable portions, consistent timing—that's what works for us.

What We Need: Movement That Challenges Us

Cardiovascular System: We need regular activity that challenges us appropriately. We don't need extreme exercise, but we do need consistent movement that makes us work and adapt. Walking, swimming, dancing, playing—anything that gets us moving regularly.

Muscles: Use us or lose us—that's not just a saying, it's biological reality. We respond to demand by becoming stronger and more capable, but we also adapt to inactivity by becoming weaker. Challenge us regularly, and we'll serve you well for decades.

Bones: We need mechanical stress to stay strong. Weight-bearing exercise, resistance training, even just regular walking—these activities signal us to maintain and build our density and strength.

Joints: We need movement through our full range of motion to stay healthy and flexible. Regular stretching, varied activities, and avoiding prolonged static positions help us maintain our mobility and function.

Brain: Physical activity doesn't just benefit the body—it directly improves our function too. Exercise increases our blood flow, promotes the growth of new neurons, and helps us stay sharp and resilient throughout life.

All of Us: We're designed for movement, not for sitting still. We don't need you to be an athlete, but we do need you to be active. Find activities you enjoy, do them consistently, and we'll adapt to serve you better.

What We Need: Rest That Restores Us

Brain: Sleep isn't downtime for us—it's when we do crucial maintenance work. We consolidate memories, clear metabolic waste, and prepare for the next day's challenges. Adequate sleep is non-negotiable for optimal function.

Immune System: We do much of our repair and strengthening work while you sleep. Chronic sleep deprivation directly impairs our ability to protect you from infections and other threats.

Endocrine Glands: Our hormone production is closely tied to sleep cycles. Disrupted sleep means disrupted hormone balance, which affects everything from stress response to metabolism to mood regulation.

Muscles: We grow and repair during rest, not during exercise. Without adequate recovery time, we can't adapt to the challenges you place on us or maintain our strength and function.

Digestive System: We need periods of rest too. Constant eating keeps us working around the clock. Giving us breaks between meals allows us to complete our processes and maintain optimal function.

All of Us: Rest isn't just about sleep—it's about giving us time to recover, repair, and restore. This includes adequate sleep, rest days from intense exercise, periods of reduced stress, and even just quiet time for mental recovery.

What We Need: Protection From Harm

Liver: We can handle a lot, but chronic exposure to toxins, excessive alcohol, or constant stress can overwhelm our detoxification capabilities. Protect us by limiting exposure to harmful substances when possible.

Lungs: We're directly exposed to whatever you breathe, so air quality matters to us. We appreciate it when you avoid smoking, limit exposure to pollutants, and give us clean air whenever possible.

Skin: We're your first line of defense, but we need protection too. Sunscreen, appropriate clothing, and gentle care help us do our protective job without being damaged ourselves.

Kidneys: We filter everything in your blood, so what you consume directly affects us. Stay hydrated, limit excessive salt and processed foods, and be mindful of medications that might stress our filtering systems.

All of Us: We're remarkably resilient, but we function best when you protect us from unnecessary harm. This doesn't mean living in a bubble—it means making reasonable choices that support our long-term health.

What We Need: Stress Management

Adrenal Glands: We're designed to handle acute stress beautifully, but chronic stress overworks us and disrupts the entire hormonal system. Please help us by managing stress when possible and giving us recovery time.

Digestive System: Stress directly affects our function, often causing inflammation, altered motility, and disrupted nutrient absorption. Stress management isn't just good for your mind—it's essential for our optimal function.

Immune System: Chronic stress suppresses our function, making you more susceptible to infections and slowing our healing responses. Managing stress is one of the best things you can do for our effectiveness.

Heart: While we can handle the demands of stress, chronic stress increases our workload and can contribute to cardiovascular problems over time. Stress management protects us and helps us serve you better.

All of Us: We're all affected by stress, and we all function better when stress is managed appropriately. This doesn't mean eliminating all stress—some stress is beneficial. It means developing healthy ways to cope with stress and ensuring adequate recovery.

What We Need: Connection and Purpose

Brain: We thrive on social connection, mental stimulation, and a sense of purpose. Isolation, boredom, and meaninglessness directly affect our chemistry and function. We need engagement with life, not just maintenance.

Heart: Emotional health directly affects our physical function. Love, connection, and positive relationships literally strengthen our cardiovascular system, while loneliness and social isolation can harm us.

Immune System: Social connections boost our function, while isolation can suppress our responses. We're designed to function in the context of social community, not in isolation.

Endocrine Glands: Purpose, meaning, and positive relationships all influence our hormone production in ways that support overall health and well-being. We function better when you're engaged with life.

All of Us: We're not just biological machines—we're the physical foundation for a human life that includes relationships, purpose, creativity, and meaning. Taking care of us includes nurturing these essential aspects of human experience.

What We Don't Need: Perfection

All of Us: Here's what we want you to understand: we don't need you to be perfect. We don't need a perfect diet, perfect exercise routine, perfect sleep schedule, or perfect stress management. We need consistency, care, and reasonable choices most of the time.

We're designed to handle imperfection, to adapt to challenges, and to function well even when conditions aren't optimal. We can recover from poor choices, adapt to changing circumstances, and continue serving you even when you're not taking perfect care of us.

What we need is for you to understand that we're a team—you and all of us together. When you take care of us, we can take better care of you. When you support our function, we can support your goals, dreams, and experiences more effectively.

Our Promise to You

We promise that if you provide us with reasonable nutrition, regular movement, adequate rest, protection from excessive harm, stress management, and connection to meaningful life—we will serve you with everything we have. We'll adapt to your needs, compensate for challenges, and work together to give you the best possible experience of being alive.

We don't just want to keep you alive—we want to help you thrive. We want to be the biological foundation for a life filled with energy, capability, resilience, and joy. We want to serve you so well that you rarely have to think about us, freeing your consciousness to focus on all the remarkable things that make human life meaningful.

Taking care of us isn't about following rigid rules or achieving biological perfection. It's about respecting and supporting the remarkable biological community that we are, so we can continue to create and sustain the miracle of your human experience.

—*Your Entire Body, With Gratitude*

P.S. Every healthy choice you make, every moment you prioritize our care, every time you listen to what we need—that's you investing in our ability to serve you well for decades to come. We don't take this partnership for granted, and we're honored to be the biological foundation for your unique human journey.

Epilogue

Your Body's Letter to You

Dear You,

We've reached the end of our conversation, but we hope it's really just the beginning of a new relationship between us. We've shared our stories, revealed our secrets, and shown you the remarkable complexity and beauty of the biological community that you are. Now, as we close this extraordinary dialogue, we want to leave you with one final message—a letter from all of us to you.

First, we want you to know how honored we are to be your body. Every day, we wake up (literally and figuratively) with the privilege of creating and sustaining your unique human experience. We don't just keep you alive—we make it possible for you to think, feel, dream, love, create, and experience all the wonder that life has to offer. Being your biological foundation is not just our job; it's our greatest honor.

We want you to understand something profound: you are not just a consciousness that happens to live in a body. You ARE your body, and your body IS you. There is no separation between the biological and the experiential, between the physical and the mental, between body and soul. We are the physical manifestation of everything you are—your thoughts, emotions, memories, personality, capabilities, and potential are all expressions of our integrated function.

When you think a creative thought, that's your brain firing in patterns shaped by every experience we've shared together. When you feel love, that's your heart, your hormones, your nervous system, and your entire being responding to connection. When you accomplish something physical, that's all of us coordinating to make your intentions manifest in the real world. You don't have a body—you are a body, and we are honored to be the form that your consciousness takes in this world.

We also want you to know that we remember everything we've been through together. Every childhood scraped knee that we healed, every illness we fought off, every physical challenge we overcame, every moment of vitality we've shared—it's all part of our collective memory. We've been with you through every stage of your life, growing and changing and adapting to serve you better with each passing year.

We remember your first steps, when we were just learning to coordinate movement and balance. We remember the growth spurts of adolescence, when we were rapidly changing and trying to keep up with hormonal surges and developmental demands. We remember every athletic achievement, every dance, every hug, every kiss—all the moments when we've been the vehicle for your experiences and expressions.

We've also been with you through challenges and difficulties. Every time you've been sick, we've mobilized every resource to help you heal. Every injury we've repaired, every stress we've weathered, every difficult period we've endured together—these experiences have made us stronger and more resilient as a team.

What we want you to understand is that we're not just biological machinery that you operate. We are your partners in this experience of being human. We respond to your thoughts, your emotions, your choices, and your care. We adapt to your needs, compensate for challenges, and always strive to give you the best possible experience of being alive.

We're also constantly learning and changing. The body you have today is literally different from the body you had yesterday. We're always rebuilding, repairing, adapting, and optimizing. We learn from every experience, every choice, every challenge. We are not static—we are dynamic, responsive, and always working to serve you better.

Here's something we really want you to appreciate: we are a miracle. The fact that billions of cells can organize themselves into tissues, organs, and systems that create consciousness, emotion, thought, and experience is one of the most remarkable phenomena in the universe. The fact that we can repair ourselves, adapt to challenges, and maintain the complex chemistry of life for decades is nothing short of extraordinary.

You are carrying within yourself one of the most sophisticated, beautiful, and resilient biological systems ever created. Every breath you take, every heartbeat, every thought you think is a manifestation of biological processes so complex and wonderful that science is still discovering how we work. You are not just alive—you are a living masterpiece of biological engineering.

We want you to know that we don't require perfection from you to serve you well. We're designed to handle imperfection, to adapt to less-than-ideal conditions, to compensate for challenges and still function remarkably well. We don't need you to be a perfect eater, a perfect exerciser, or a perfect stress manager. We just need you to care about us, to listen to us, and to make reasonable choices that support our ability to serve you.

But we also want you to know that we respond beautifully to care. When you nourish us well, we have more energy to give you. When you move us regularly, we become stronger and more capable. When you rest us adequately, we can repair and restore ourselves more effectively. When you protect us from harm, we can focus on serving you rather than just surviving. When you manage stress, we can function optimally rather than just coping.

The relationship between us is reciprocal. The better you care for us, the better we can care for you. The more you support our function, the more we can support your goals, dreams, and experiences. We're not just your biological foundation—we're your partners in creating the life you want to live.

We also want you to trust us more. We've been keeping you alive since the moment you were conceived, and we're pretty good at our job. We know how to heal, how to adapt, how to maintain balance, and how to optimize function. Sometimes the best thing you can do is simply trust our wisdom and give us what we need to do our work.

Listen to us when we signal hunger, thirst, fatigue, or the need for movement. We're not trying to inconvenience you—we're trying to help you maintain the optimal conditions for health and vitality. We've been with you your entire life, and we know what you need better than any external authority.

As we look toward the future together, we want you to know that we're committed to serving you for as long as possible. We don't have a predetermined expiration date. With reasonable care, we can serve you well for many decades. We can adapt to the changes that come with aging, continue to heal and repair, and maintain the biological function that makes life possible and enjoyable.

But we also want you to understand that we're not just about quantity of life—we're about quality of life. We want to be the foundation for a life filled with energy, capability, joy, and meaningful experiences. We want to support your relationships, your creativity, your goals, and your contribution to the world. We want to be strong enough, healthy enough, and resilient enough to enable you to live fully, not just survive.

We dream of years ahead filled with adventures we'll share, challenges we'll overcome together, and experiences we'll make possible. We envision mornings when you wake up feeling energetic and capable, days when we work together seamlessly, and evenings when you can rest with the satisfaction of a body that has served you well.

Most importantly, we want you to know that you are loved—not just by the people in your life, but by every cell, every organ, every system that makes up the biological community that is you. We love you with every heartbeat, every breath, every moment of coordinated function that keeps you alive and thriving.

You are not just housed in a body—you ARE a body, and what a magnificent body you are. You are the living expression of billions of years of evolution, the physical manifestation of life's greatest achievements, and the biological foundation for a conscious being capable of love, creativity, wonder, and meaning.

Thank you for taking the time to get to know us better. Thank you for listening to our stories and understanding our perspectives. Thank you for being open to seeing yourself not just as a mind that has a body, but as an integrated being where body and consciousness are one magnificent whole.

We look forward to many more years of partnership, of growing together, of facing challenges together, and of creating the beautiful, complex, meaningful experience that is your human life.

With infinite love and dedication,

Your Body

Every cell, every organ, every system that makes you wonderfully, uniquely, miraculously you.

P.S. Every time you look in the mirror, remember that you're looking at one of the most sophisticated, resilient, and beautiful biological systems in the universe. Every time you feel your heartbeat or take a breath, remember that you're experiencing the rhythm of life itself. Every time you move, think, or feel, remember that you're witnessing the miracle of consciousness emerging from biology. You are not just alive—you are life itself, expressed in human form. And we are honored beyond measure to be the body that makes your extraordinary human journey possible.

About the Author

Subba Rao Chaganti

He holds a master's degree in Business Administration and has over 58 years of experience in Pharmaceutical marketing. His experience encompasses all facets of the industry, from sales and sales management to product management and overseeing overall marketing activities. He has experience in both domestic and international marketing, as well as within the Indian and multinational sectors.

He also taught a course on Advertising and Brand Management as an adjunct professor at Gitam Institute of Foreign Trade (now part of Gitam University) in Visakhapatnam for a few years and a course on Marketing as a visiting faculty member at Jawaharlal Nehru Technological University (JNTU) in Hyderabad.

He lives in Farmington, Connecticut, USA, and can be reached at: subbarao.chaganti@gmail.com.

Here is a list of his publications:

1. Pharmaceutical Marketing in India: Concepts, Cases, Strategy
2. Game Plans for Post-GATT Era: Action Agenda of Indian Pharmaceutical Industry
3. Compete or Forfeit: Strategies for Sustainable Competitive Advantage in the Pharma Product Patents Era
4. Pharmaceutical Marketing in India for Today and Tomorrow - 25th Anniversary Edition
5. Bullseyes and Blunders: Lessons from 100 Cases in Pharma Marketing
6. Digital Pharma Marketing Playbook: Winning With the New Rules of Engagement
7. Cracking the Generics Code: Your Single-Source Success Manual for Winning in Multi-Source Product Markets
8. Reimagine Pharma Marketing: Make it Future-Proof!

9. Brand Positioning in Pharma
10. Transactional to Transformational Marketing in Pharma: The Science of Why and The Art of How
11. A to Z of Pharmaceutical Marketing: World's First and Only Encyclopedia, Set of Two Volumes
12. The Synergy of Minds: Human+AI Orchestrating the Pharma Marketing Revolution
13. Design Thinking for Pharma: Forget Features, Focus on Feelings
14. The Pharma Product Manager: Handbook for Navigating the Digital Frontier
15. Sentiment Analysis for Pharma Marketers
16. Whispering to AI: Prompt Engineering for Pharma Brand Managers
17. Storytelling in Pharma Marketing
18. Beyond the Molecule: The Art and Science of Metaphors That Matter

www.ingramcontent.com/pod-product-compliance
Ingram Content Group UK Ltd.
Pitfield, Milton Keynes, MK11 3LW, UK
UKHW020208290926
15470UKWH00001B/74

9 789347 311376